Congressional
Research
Service

Federal Research and Development Funding: FY2014

John F. Sargent Jr., Coordinator
Specialist in Science and Technology Policy

November 5, 2013

Congressional Research Service

7-5700

www.crs.gov

R43086

CRS Report for Congress ————————————————————

Summary

Congress has received President Obama's budget request for FY2014, which includes $142.773 billion for research and development (R&D), a $1.861 billion (1.3%) increase from the FY2012 actual funding level of $140.912 billion. The request represents the President's R&D priorities; Congress may opt to agree with part or all of the request, or may express different priorities through the appropriations process. In particular, Congress will play a central role in determining the extent to which the federal R&D investment can grow in the context of increased pressure on discretionary spending and how available funding will be prioritized and allocated. Low or negative growth in the overall R&D investment may require movement of resources across disciplines, programs, or agencies to address priorities.

Funding for R&D is highly concentrated in a few departments. Under President Obama's request, seven federal agencies would receive 95.3% of total federal R&D funding, with the Department of Defense (47.8%) and the Department of Health and Human Services (22.4%, primarily for the National Institutes of Health) accounting for more than 70% of total federal R&D funding.

Among the largest changes proposed in the President's request, the R&D budget of the Department of Defense would fall by $4.625 billion (6.3%), while R&D funding for the Department of Commerce's National Institute of Standards and Technology (NIST) would increase by $1.428 billion. The NIST growth is fueled by increases in funding for its core research laboratories and by the establishment of the National Network for Manufacturing Innovation with $1 billion in mandatory funding. The NNMI seeks to promote the development of manufacturing technologies with broad applications.

President Obama has requested increases in the R&D budgets of NIST, the National Science Foundation, and the Department of Energy's Office of Science that were targeted for doubling over 7 years, from their FY2006 levels, by the America COMPETES Act, and over 10 years by the America COMPETES Reauthorization Act of 2010. The FY2014 request breaks with President Obama's earlier budgets, which explicitly stated the goal of doubling funding for these accounts over their FY2006 aggregate level. Instead the Office of Science and Technology Policy asserts that the FY2014 request "maintains the President's commitment to increase funding for research at these three science agencies." The President's FY2014 request sets a pace that would result in doubling of the FY2006 level over a period of more than 17 years.

The President's request continues support for three multi-agency R&D initiatives in FY2014, proposing $1.704 billion for the National Nanotechnology Initiative, a reduction of $159 million (8.6%) over FY2012, due primarily to reductions in NNI funding at DOD and NSF; $3.968 billion for the Networking and Information Technology Research and Development program, an increase of $159 million (4.2%) over FY2012; and $2.652 billion for the U.S. Global Change Research Program, an increase of $151 million (6.0%) over FY2012.

On October 16, 2013, the House and Senate passed the Continuing Appropriations Act, 2014 (H.R. 2775), which was subsequently signed into law (P.L. 113-46) by President Obama on October 17, 2013. The act provides continuing appropriations for FY2014 generally at the levels of, and under the terms and conditions of, FY2013 funding as reduced by sequestration, until whichever of the following first occurs: (1) enactment of an appropriation for any project or activity provided for in it; (2) enactment of the applicable appropriations Act for FY2014 without any provision for such project or activity; or (3) January 15, 2014. In recent years, Congress has used a variety of mechanisms to complete the annual appropriations process after the start of the fiscal year. This may affect agencies' execution of their R&D budgets, including delaying or canceling some planned R&D and equipment acquisition.

Contents

Figures

Tables

Contacts

Overview

The 113th Congress continues to take a strong interest in the health of the U.S. research and development (R&D) enterprise and in providing support for federal R&D activities. The federal government has played an important role in supporting R&D efforts that have led to scientific breakthroughs and new technologies, from jet aircraft and the Internet to communications satellites and defenses against disease. However, widespread concerns about the federal debt and recent and projected federal budget deficits are driving difficult decisions involving prioritization of R&D within the context of the entire federal budget and among competing priorities within the federal R&D portfolio.

The U.S. government supports a broad range of scientific and engineering R&D. Its purposes include addressing specific concerns such as national defense, health, safety, the environment, and energy security; advancing knowledge generally; developing the scientific and engineering workforce; and strengthening U.S. innovation and competitiveness in the global economy. Most of the R&D funded by the federal government is performed in support of the unique missions of the funding agencies.

Congress will play a central role in defining the nation's R&D priorities as it makes decisions about the size and distribution of R&D funding—overall, within agencies, and for specific programs. Some Members of Congress have expressed concerns about the level of federal funding (for R&D as for other purposes) in light of the current federal fiscal condition, deficit, and debt. As Congress acts to complete the FY2014 appropriations process it faces two overarching issues: the extent to which the federal R&D investment can grow in the context of increased pressure on discretionary spending and how available funding will be prioritized and allocated. Low or negative growth in the overall R&D investment may require movement of resources across disciplines, programs, or agencies to address priorities.

President Obama released his proposed FY2014 budget on April 10, 2013. Since FY2013 final appropriations figures (post-sequestration) were not yet available, the President's budget compared the FY2014 request generally to FY2012 funding rather than to FY2013 funding. This report also uses FY2012 as the base comparison year; in some cases the analysis of growth rates is also presented in terms of compound annual growth rates (CAGRs).[1]

This report provides government-wide, multi-agency, and individual agency analyses of the President's FY2014 request as it relates to R&D and related activities. The President's budget seeks $142.773 billion for R&D in FY2014, a 1.3% increase (0.7% CAGR) over the actual FY2012 R&D funding level of $140.912 billion.[2] Adjusted for inflation, the President's FY2014 R&D request represents a decrease of 2.6% from the FY2012 level (1.3% CAGR).[3]

---

[1] CAGR provides a measure of annual growth. CAGR is a calculated growth rate which, if applied year after year to a beginning amount, reaches a specified final amount.

[2] Funding levels included in this document are in current dollars unless otherwise noted. Inflation diminishes the purchasing power of federal R&D funds, so an increase that falls short of the inflation rate may reduce real purchasing power.

[3] As calculated by CRS using the GDP (chained) price index from Table 10.1, Gross Domestic Product and Deflators Used in the Historical Tables: 1940–2018, from the President's FY2014 budget, http://www.whitehouse.gov/sites/default/files/omb/budget/fy2014/assets/hist10z1 xls.

Among its provisions, the R&D funding in the President's proposed FY2014 budget maintains an emphasis on increasing support for the physical sciences and engineering, an effort consistent with the intent of the America COMPETES Act (P.L. 110-69) and the America COMPETES Reauthorization Act of 2010 (P.L. 111-358). These acts seek to achieve this objective by authorizing increased funding for accounts at three agencies with a strong R&D emphasis in these disciplines: the Department of Energy Office of Science, the National Science Foundation, and the Department of Commerce National Institute of Standards and Technology's core laboratory research and R&D facilities construction funding (collectively referred to as the "targeted accounts"). Appropriations provided to these agencies have fallen short of the levels authorized in P.L. 110-69. (See "Multiagency R&D Initiatives" for detailed information.)

More broadly, in a 2009 speech before members of the National Academy of Sciences, President Obama put forth a goal of increasing the national (public and private) investment in R&D to more than 3% of the U.S. gross domestic product (GDP). President Obama did not provide details on how this goal might be achieved (e.g., how much would be funded through increases in direct federal R&D funding or through indirect mechanisms such as the research and experimentation (R&E) tax credit).[4] Doing so likely would require a substantial increase in government and/or corporate R&D spending. When President Obama set forth the goal in 2009, total U.S. R&D expenditures were $404 billion, or approximately 2.90% of GDP, so reaching the 3% goal would have required an increase of 3.6% in national R&D spending per dollar of GDP. Since then, however, GDP has grown faster than R&D. As a result, total estimated U.S. R&D expenditures of $414 billion in 2011 accounted for a smaller fraction (2.7%) of GDP than in 2009. Therefore, reaching the 3% goal in 2011 would have required an increase of 9.4% in national R&D spending per dollar of GDP.[5]

Analysis of federal R&D funding is complicated by several factors, such as inconsistency among agencies in the reporting of R&D and the inclusion of R&D in accounts with non-R&D activities. As a result of these and other factors, the R&D agency figures reported by the White House Office of Management and Budget (OMB) and White House Office of Science and Technology Policy (OSTP), including those shown in **Table 1**, may differ somewhat from the agency budget analyses that appear later in this report.

Federal R&D Funding Perspectives

Federal R&D funding can be analyzed from a variety of perspectives that provide different insights. The following sections examine the data viewed by agency, by the character of the work supported, by a combination of these two perspectives, and by defense-related and nondefense-related R&D.

---

[4] The research and experimentation tax credit is frequently referred to as the research and development tax credit or R&D tax credit, through the credit does not apply to development expenditures. For additional information about the R&E tax credit, see CRS Report RL31181, *Research Tax Credit: Current Law and Policy Issues for the 113th Congress*, by Gary Guenther.

[5] GDP figures from Bureau of Economic Analysis, *Survey of Current Business*, 31 May 2012; R&D figures from National Science Foundation, National Center for Science and Engineering Statistics, *National Patterns of R&D Resources* (annual series).

By Agency

The authorization and appropriations process views federal R&D funding primarily from the perspective of individual agencies and programs. **Table 1** provides data on R&D by agency for FY2012 (actual), FY2013 (estimate), and FY2014 (request) as reported by OMB. This table will be updated as post-sequestration funding data become available.

Under President Obama's FY2014 budget request, seven federal agencies would receive 95.3% of total federal R&D funding: Department of Defense (DOD), 47.8%; Department of Health and Human Services (HHS) (primarily the National Institutes of Health), 22.4%; Department of Energy (DOE), 8.9%; National Aeronautics and Space Administration (NASA), 8.1%; National Science Foundation (NSF), 4.3%; Department of Commerce (DOC), 1.9%; and Department of Agriculture (USDA), 1.8%. This report provides an analysis of the R&D budget requests for these agencies, as well as for the Department of Homeland Security (DHS), Department of the Interior (DOI), Department of Transportation (DOT), and the Environmental Protection Agency (EPA). In total, these 11 agencies account for 98% of current and requested federal R&D funding.

The largest agency R&D increases in the President's FY2014 request, compared with the FY2012 levels, are for DOE, $1.928 billion (17.8%); DOC, $1.428 billion (113.9%);[6] DHS, $893 million (185.7%); HHS, $669 million (2.1%); NSF, $512 million (9.1%); and NASA, $290 million (2.6%). Under the President's FY2014 budget request, DOD R&D funding would be reduced by $4.625 billion (6.3%) and EPA R&D by $8 million (1.4%).

Table 1. Federal Research and Development Funding by Agency, FY2012-FY2014

(Budget authority, dollar amounts in millions)

Department/Agency	FY2012 Actual	FY2013 Estimate[a]	FY2014 Request	Change, 2012-2014		
				Dollar	Percent	CAGR
DOD	$72,916		$68,291	$−4,625	−6.3%	−3.2%
HHS	31,377		32,046	669	2.1%	1.1%
DOE	10,811		12,739	1,928	17.8%	8.6%
NASA	11,315		11,605	290	2.6%	1.3%
NSF	5,636		6,148	512	9.1%	4.4%
DOC	1,254		2,682	1,428	113.9%	46.2%
USDA	2,331		2,523	192	8.2%	4.0%
DHS	481		1,374	893	185.7%	69.0%

---

[6] The Department of Commerce total includes the mandatory funding proposal for the National Network for Manufacturing Innovation at the National Institute of Standards and Technology. This program is discussed in the DOC NIST section of this report. Mandatory spending is typically provided in permanent or multi-year appropriations contained in the authorizing law, and therefore, the funding becomes available automatically each year, without legislative action by Congress. For additional information on mandatory spending, see CRS Report RL33074, *Mandatory Spending Since 1962*, by Mindy R. Levit and D. Andrew Austin.

Department/Agency	FY2012 Actual	FY2013 Estimate[a]	FY2014 Request	Change, 2012-2014		
				Dollar	Percent	CAGR
Department of Veterans Affairs	1,160		1,172	12	1.0%	0.5%
DOI	820		963	143	17.4%	8.4%
DOT	921		942	21	2.3%	1.1%
EPA	568		560	−8	−1.4%	−0.7%
Other	1,322		1,728	406	30.7%	14.3%
Total	**140,912**		**142,773**	**1,861**	**1.3%**	**0.7%**

Source: Executive Office of the President, OMB, Analytical Perspectives, Budget of the United States Government, Fiscal Year 2014, Table 21-1.

Notes: Totals may differ from the sum of the components due to rounding.

a. FY2013 post-sequestration funding data will be added when available.

By Character of Work, Facilities, and Equipment

Federal R&D funding can also be examined by the character of work it supports—basic research, applied research, or development—and by funding provided for construction of R&D facilities and acquisition of major R&D equipment. (See **Table 2**.) President Obama's FY2014 request includes $33.162 billion for basic research, up $1.422 million (4.5%) from FY2012 (2.2% CAGR); $34.963 billion for applied research, up $3.345 billion (10.6%) from FY2012 (5.2% CAGR); $71.463 billion for development, down $3.781 billion (5.0%) from FY2012 (2.5% CAGR); and $3.185 billion for facilities and equipment, up $875 million (37.9%) from FY2012 (17.4% CAGR).

Table 2. Federal Research and Development Funding by Character of Work and Facilities and Equipment, FY2012-FY2014

(Budget authority, dollar amounts in millions)

	FY2012 Actual	FY2013 Estimate[a]	FY2014 Request	Change, 2012-2014		
				Dollar	Percent	CAGR
Basic research	31,740		33,162	$1,422	4.5%	2.2%
Applied research	31,618		34,963	3,345	10.6%	5.2%
Development	75,244		71,463	−3,781	−5.0%	−2.5%
Facilities and Equipment	2,310		3,185	875	37.9%	17.4%
Total	**140,912**		**142,773**	**1,861**	**1.3%**	**0.7%**

Source: Executive Office of the President, OMB, *Analytical Perspectives, Budget of the United States Government, Fiscal Year 2014*, Table 21-1.

Notes: Totals may differ from the sum of the components due to rounding.

a. FY2013 post-sequestration funding data will be added when available.

By Agency and Character of Work Combined

Combining these perspectives, federal R&D funding can be viewed in terms of each agency's contribution to basic research, applied research, development, and facilities and equipment. (See **Table 3**.) The overall federal R&D budget reflects a wide range of national priorities, from supporting advances in spaceflight to developing new and affordable sources of energy. These priorities and the mission of each agency contribute, in part, to the composition of that agency's R&D spending (i.e., the allocation between basic research, applied research, development, and facilities and equipment). In the President's FY2014 budget request, the Department of Health and Human Services, primarily the National Institutes of Health (NIH), accounts for nearly half of all federal funding for basic research.[7] HHS is also the largest funder of applied research, accounting for about 45% of all federally funded applied research in the President's FY2014 budget request.[8] DOD is the primary federal agency funder of development, accounting for 86.1% of total federal development funding in the President's FY2014 budget request.[9]

The federal government is the nation's largest supporter of basic research, funding 53.3% of U.S. basic research in 2011, primarily because the private sector asserts it cannot capture an adequate return on long-term fundamental research investments. In contrast, industry funded 22.5% of U.S. basic research in 2011 (with state governments, universities, and other non-profit organizations funding the remaining 24.2%).[10] In contrast to basic research, industry is the primary funder of applied research in the United States, accounting for an estimated 51.2% in 2011, while the federal government accounted for an estimated 38.8%.[11] Industry also provides the vast majority of funding for development. Industry accounted for an estimated 74.6% in 2011, while the federal government provided an estimated 23.7%.[12]

---

[7] Executive Office of the President, Office of Management and Budget, *Analytical Perspectives, Budget of the United States Government, Fiscal Year 2014,* Table 21-1.

[8] Executive Office of the President, Office of Management and Budget, *Analytical Perspectives, Budget of the United States Government, Fiscal Year 2014,* Table 21-1.

[9] Executive Office of the President, Office of Management and Budget, *Analytical Perspectives, Budget of the United States Government, Fiscal Year 2014,* Table 21-1.

[10] National Science Foundation, National Center for Science and Engineering Statistics, 2013, *National Patterns of R&D Resources: 2010–11 Data Update,* NSF 13-318, http://www.nsf.gov/statistics/nsf13318/.

[11] National Science Foundation, National Center for Science and Engineering Statistics, 2013, *National Patterns of R&D Resources: 2010–11 Data Update,* NSF 13-318, http://www.nsf.gov/statistics/nsf13318/.

[12] National Science Foundation, National Center for Science and Engineering Statistics, 2013, *National Patterns of R&D Resources: 2010–11 Data Update,* NSF 13-318, http://www.nsf.gov/statistics/nsf13318/.

Table 3. Top R&D Funding Agencies by Character of Work, Facilities, and Equipment, FY2012-FY2014

(Budget authority, dollar amounts in millions)

	FY2012 Actual	FY2013 Estimate[a]	FY2014 Request	Change, 2012 to 2014		
				Dollar	Percent	CAGR
Basic Research						
Health and Human Services	16,195		16,182	−13	−0.1%	0.0%
National Science Foundation	4,584		5,120	536	11.7%	5.7%
Energy	3,912		4,129	217	5.5%	2.7%
Applied Research						
Health and Human Services	14,933		15,660	727	4.9%	2.4%
Defense	4,728		4,602	−126	−2.7%	−1.3%
Energy	3,584		4,405	821	22.9%	10.9%
Development						
Defense	66,069		61,499	−4,570	−6.9%	−3.5%
NASA	5,344		5,135	−209	−3.9%	−2.0%
Energy	2,446		3,338	892	36.5%	16.8%
Facilities and Equipment						
Energy	869		867	−2	−0.2%	−0.1%
Homeland Security	97		778	681	702.1%	183.2%
National Science Foundation	535		548	13	2.4%	1.2%

Source: Executive Office of the President, OMB, *Analytical Perspectives, Budget of the United States Government, Fiscal Year 2014,* April 10, 2013.

Note: Top three funding agencies in each category based on FY2014 request.

a.   FY2013 post-sequestration funding data will be added when available.

Defense-Related and Nondefense-Related R&D

Federal R&D funding is also characterized as defense-related or nondefense-related. Defense-related R&D is provided for primarily by the Department of Defense, but includes some funding at the Department of Energy and the Department of Justice Federal Bureau of Investigation. Defense-related R&D has generally provided for more than half of total federal R&D funding for the past two decades, fluctuating between 50% and 70%. Defense related R&D grew from 52.7% of total federal R&D funding in FY2001 to 60.5% in FY2008 and has since declined. The President's request for FY2014 includes $73.2 billion in defense-related R&D funding, or about 51.2% of the total R&D request.

Multiagency R&D Initiatives

Although this report focuses primarily on the R&D activities of individual agencies, President Obama's FY2014 budget request supports several multiagency R&D initiatives. The following sections discuss several of these.

Efforts to Double Certain R&D Accounts

In 2006, President Bush announced the American Competitiveness Initiative which, in part, sought to increase federal funding for physical sciences and engineering research by doubling funding over 10 years (FY2006-FY2016) for targeted accounts at three agencies: NSF, DOE Office of Science, and the scientific and technical research and services (STRS) and construction of research facilities (CRF) accounts at the DOC National Institute of Standards and Technology.

In 2007, Congress authorized substantial increases for these targeted accounts under the America COMPETES Act (P.L. 110-69), which set the combined authorization levels for these accounts for FY2008-FY2010 at a seven-year doubling pace.[13] However, funding provided for these agencies in the Consolidated Appropriations Act, 2008 (P.L. 110-161), the Omnibus Appropriations Act, 2009 (P.L. 111-8), and the Consolidated Appropriations Act, 2010 (P.L. 111-117) fell below these targets.[14] (See **Table 4** for individual and aggregate appropriations for the targeted accounts.)

In 2010, Congress passed the America COMPETES Reauthorization Act of 2010 (P.L. 111-358) which, among other things, authorized appropriations levels for the targeted accounts for FY2011-FY2013.[15] The aggregate authorization levels in this act for the targeted accounts are consistent with an 11-year doubling path, slower than the America COMPETES Act's 7-year doubling path. Moreover, aggregate FY2012 funding for the targeted accounts was approximately $12.529 billion, $1.631 billion less than authorized in the act, setting a pace to double over 17 years from the FY2006 level—more than twice the length of time originally envisioned in the 2007 America COMPETES Act and more than half longer than the doubling period established by the America COMPETES Reauthorization Act of 2010.[16]

In his FY2014 budget, President Obama is requesting $13.532 billion in aggregate funding for the targeted accounts, an increase of $1.003 billion (8.0%) above the enacted FY2012 aggregate funding level of $12.529 billion.

---

[13] CRS Report R41951, *An Analysis of Efforts to Double Federal Funding for Physical Sciences and Engineering Research*, by John F. Sargent Jr.

[14] In 2009, the American Recovery and Reinvestment Act of 2009 (P.L. 111-5) provided supplemental funding for several of the targeted accounts (approximately $5.202 billion). This raised funding for the accounts above the target levels in that year.

[15] For additional information, see CRS Report R41231, *America COMPETES Reauthorization Act of 2010 (H.R. 5116) and the America COMPETES Act (P.L. 110-69): Selected Policy Issues*, coordinated by Heather B. Gonzalez.

[16] All doubling path calculations in this report use FY2006 as the baseline. For additional information on the doubling effort, see CRS Report R41951, *An Analysis of Efforts to Double Federal Funding for Physical Sciences and Engineering Research*, by John F. Sargent Jr.

In light of budget constraints, the future of the doubling path appears to be in question. In his FY2010 *Plan for Science and Innovation,* President Obama stated that he, like President Bush, would seek to double funding for basic research over 10 years (FY2006 to FY2016) at the ACI agencies.[17] In his FY2011 budget documents, President Obama extended the period over which he intended to double these agencies' budgets to 11 years (FY2006 to FY2017).[18] The FY2013 budget request, like the FY2012 budget request, reiterated President Obama's intention to double funding for the targeted accounts from their FY2006 levels but did not specify the length of time over which the doubling is to take place. President Obama's 2014 budget expresses a commitment to increasing funding for the targeted accounts, but does not commit to doubling, remaining silent on this goal and timeframe. In addition, the Office of Management and Budget's Public Budget Database, published as part of the President's FY2014 request, includes projections of budget authority for the targeted accounts through FY2018; projected FY2018 funding for the targeted accounts sets a doubling pace of approximately 19 years.

Table 4. Funding for Accounts Targeted for Doubling FY2006-FY2014

(budget authority, in millions of current dollars)

Agency	FY2006 Actual	FY2007 Actual	FY2008 Actual	FY2009 Actual	FY2009 ARRA	FY2010 Actual	FY2011 Actual	FY2012 Actual	FY2013 Est.a	FY2014 Req.
NSF	5,646	5,884	6,084	6,469	2,402	6,972	6,913b	7,033		7,626
DOE/Office of Science	3,632	3,837	4,083	4,807	1,633	4,964	4,843	4,874		5,153
NIST/core researchc	395	434	441	472	220	515	497	567		694
NIST/facilities	174	59	161	172	360	147	70	55		60
Total	9,846	10,214	10,768	11,920	4,615	12,598	12,323	12,529		13,533

Source: NIST, budget requests for FY2008-FY2014, available at http://www.nist.gov/public_affairs/budget/index.cfm; DOE, budget requests for FY2008-FY2014, available at http://www.cfo.doe.gov/crorgcf30.htm; NSF, budget requests for FY2008-FY2014 available at http://www.nsf.gov/about/budget.

Notes: Totals may differ from the sum of the components due to rounding.

a.   FY2013 post-sequestration funding data will be added when available.

b.   Includes $54 million transferred to the U.S. Coast Guard for icebreaking services (per P.L. 112-10).

c.   NIST core research is performed under its scientific and technical research and services (STRS) account.

Figure 1 shows total funding for the targeted accounts as a percentage of their FY2006 funding level, and illustrates how actual (FY2006-FY2012), requested (FY2007-FY2014), projected (FY2015-FY2018), and authorized appropriations (FY2008-FY2013) compare to different doubling rates using FY2006 as the base year. The thick black line at the top of the chart is at 200%, the doubling level. The data used in **Figure 1** are in current dollars, not constant dollars, thus the effect of inflation on the purchasing power of these funds is not taken into consideration.

---

[17] Executive Office of the President, Office of Science and Technology Policy, *The President's Plan for Science and Innovation: Doubling Funding for Key Basic Research Agencies in the 2010 Budget,* May 7, 2009, http://www.whitehouse.gov/files/documents/ostp/budget/doubling.pdf.

[18] Executive Office of the President, Office of Science and Technology Policy, *The President's Plan for Science and Innovation: Doubling Funding for Key Basic Research Agencies in the 2011 Budget,* February 1, 2010, http://www.whitehouse.gov/sites/default/files/doubling%2011%20final.pdf.

**Figure 1. Funding for Accounts Targeted for Doubling:
Appropriations, Authorizations, and Requests versus Selected Doubling Rates**

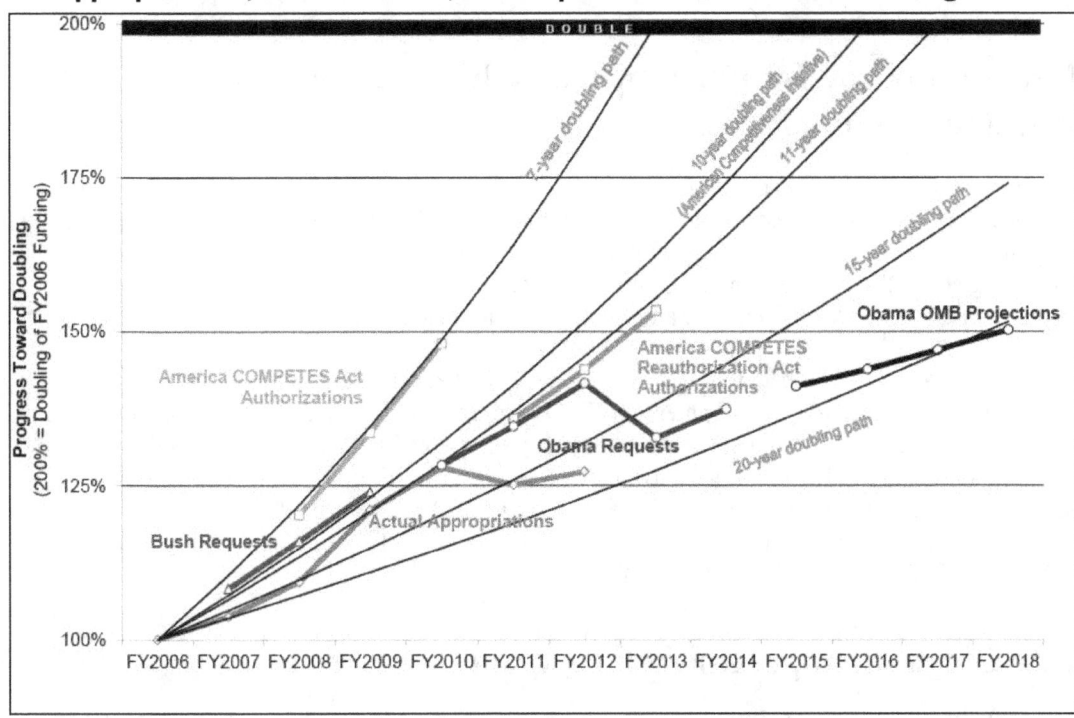

Source: Prepared by the Congressional Research Service (CRS) using agency budget justifications for FY2008-FY2014; the President's FY2014 budget request; and agency authorization levels from the America COMPETES Act (P.L. 110-69) and the America COMPETES Reauthorization Act of 2010 (P.L. 111-358).

Notes: The 7-year doubling pace represents annual increases of 10.4%, the 10-year doubling pace represents annual increases of 7.2%, the 11-year doubling pace represents annual increases of 6.5%, the 15-year doubling represents annual increases of 4.7%, and the 20-year doubling represents annual increases of 3.3%. Through compounding, these rates achieve the doubling of funding in the specified time period. The lines connecting aggregate appropriations for the targeted accounts are for illustration purposes only. Funding provided under the American Recovery and Reinvestment Act of 2009 (P.L. 111-5) is excluded from the FY2009 "Actual Appropriations" amount.

National Nanotechnology Initiative

Launched by President Clinton in his FY2001 budget request, the National Nanotechnology Initiative (NNI) is a multiagency R&D initiative advancing understanding and control of matter at the nanoscale, where the physical, chemical, and biological properties of materials differ in fundamental and useful ways from the properties of individual atoms or bulk matter.[19]

The President is requesting $1.704 billion for the NNI in FY2014, a reduction of $159 million (8.6%) from the FY2012 actual level of $1.863 billion. Among the most substantial changes in nanotechnology funding under the Administration's FY2014 request: reductions for DOD ($209 million, 49.1%) and NSF ($35 million, 7.6%), and increases for DOE ($56 million, 17.8%), DHS

---

[19] In the context of the NNI and nanotechnology, the nanoscale refers to a dimension of 1 to 100 nanometers.

($16 million, 86.5%), HHS ($8 million, 1.7%), and DOC ($7 million, 7.0%). Nanotechnology funding for other NNI agencies would remain essentially flat in FY2014.[20]

Networking and Information Technology Research and Development Program

Established by the High-Performance Computing Act of 1991 (P.L. 102-194), the Networking and Information Technology Research and Development (NITRD) program is the primary mechanism by which the federal government coordinates its unclassified networking and information technology (NIT) R&D investments in areas such as supercomputing, high-speed networking, cybersecurity, software engineering, and information management.

President Obama has requested $3.968 billion in FY2014 for the Networking and Information Technology Research and Development (NITRD) program. This is $159 million (4.2%) above the FY2012 funding level. The most substantial agency increases in NITRD funding under the Administration's FY2014 request are for the DOC (up $51 million, 42.6%), DOE (up $44 million, 8.8%), DOD (up $38 million, 3.0%), DHS (up $22 million, 40.6%), and NSF (up $11 million, 0.9%). The President's budget would reduce HHS NITRD funding by $6 million (down 1.0%) and NASA by $2 million (down 1.9%).[21]

U.S. Global Change Research Program

The U.S. Global Change Research Program (USGCRP) coordinates and integrates federal research and applications to understand, assess, predict, and respond to human-induced and natural processes of global change.

President Obama has proposed $2.652 billion for the U.S. Global Change Research Program (USGCRP) in FY2014, $151 million (6.0%) above the FY2012 estimated level of $2.501 billion. The most substantial agency increases in USGCRP funding under the Administration's FY2014 request are for NASA (up $71 million, 5.0%), DOC (up $45 million, 13.8%), DOI U.S. Geological Survey (up $13 million, 22.2%), and USDA (up $11 million, 9.8%).[22]

Materials Genome Initiative

Announced in June 2011 by President Obama, the Materials Genome Initiative is a multi-agency initiative

---

[20] Executive Office of the President, Office of Science and Technology Policy, *The 2014 Budget: A World-Leading Commitment to Science and Research—Science, Technology, Innovation, and STEM Education in the 2014 Budget*, Table 2, April 10, 2013. For additional information on the NNI, see CRS Report RL34401, *The National Nanotechnology Initiative: Overview, Reauthorization, and Appropriations Issues*, by John F. Sargent Jr.

[21] Ibid. For additional information on the NITRD program, see CRS Report RL33586, *The Federal Networking and Information Technology Research and Development Program: Background, Funding, and Activities*, by Patricia Moloney Figliola.

[22] Ibid. For additional information on the USGCRP, see CRS Report RL33817, *Climate Change: Federal Program Funding and Tax Incentives*, by Jane A. Leggett.

to create new knowledge, tools, and infrastructure with a goal of enabling U.S. industries to discover, manufacture, and deploy advanced materials twice as fast than is possible today. Agencies are currently developing implementation strategies for the Materials Genome Initiative with a focus on: (1) the creation of a materials innovation infrastructure, (2) achieving national goals with advanced materials, and (3) equipping the next generation materials workforce. Materials science funding opportunities announced in FY2012 and requested in the FY2013 budget reflect these efforts.[23]

In congressional testimony, OSTP Director John Holdren stated that the purpose of the Materials Genome Initiative is to "speed our understanding of the fundamentals of materials science, providing a wealth of practical information that American entrepreneurs and innovators will be able to use to develop new products and processes" in much the same way that the Human Genome Project accelerated a range of biological sciences by identifying and deciphering the human genetic code.[24] The President's FY2014 budget does not include a table of agency funding for the MGI, but the initiative is referred to in the Analytical Perspectives supplement to the President's budget[25] and multiple times in the National Science Foundation's *FY2014 Budget Request to Congress*.[26] Among the agencies funding MGI R&D are DOE, DOD, NSF, and NIST.

Advanced Manufacturing Partnership

In June 2011, President Obama launched the Advanced Manufacturing Partnership (AMP), an effort to bring together "industry, universities, and the Federal government to invest in emerging technologies that will create high-quality manufacturing jobs and enhance our global competitiveness."[27] Two R&D-focused components of the AMP are the National Robotics Initiative (NRI) and the National Network for Manufacturing Innovation (NNMI).

National Robotics Initiative

The National Robotics Initiative (NRI) seeks to "develop robots that work with or beside people to extend or augment human capabilities."[28] Among the goals of the program are increasing labor productivity in the manufacturing sector, assisting with dangerous and expensive missions in space, accelerating the discovery of new drugs, and improving food safety by rapidly sensing microbial contamination.[29] In FY2012, four agencies—NSF, NIH, NASA, and USDA—issued a joint solicitation to provide research funding for next-generation robotics. In addition, the Department of Defense, through multiple component agencies, is supporting the NRI through the

---

[23] E-mail correspondence between OSTP and CRS, March 14, 2012.

[24] John P. Holdren, Director, Office of Science and Technology Policy, Executive Office of the President, testimony before the Senate Committee on Commerce, Science, and Transportation, Subcommittee on Science and Space, hearing on "Keeping America Competitive Through Investments in R&D," March 6, 2012, http://commerce.senate.gov/public/?a=Files.Serve&File_id=fed566eb-e2c8-49da-aec5-f84e4045890b.

[25] Office of Management and Budget, Executive Office of the President, *Analytical Perspectives, Budget of the United States Government, Fiscal Year 2014*, p. 371.

[26] National Science Foundation, *Fiscal Year 2014 Budget of the U.S. Government*, April 10, 2013, http://www.nsf.gov/about/budget/fy2014/pdf/EntireDocument_fy2014.pdf.

[27] Ibid.

[28] Ibid.

[29] Executive Office of the President, Office of Science and Technology Policy, website, August 3, 2011, http://www.whitehouse.gov/blog/2011/08/03/supporting-president-s-national-robotics-initiative.

Defense University Research Instrumentation Program. DOD is supporting the purchase of equipment to assist in robotics research to advance defense technologies and applications, including unmanned ground, air, sea, and undersea vehicles and autonomous systems.[30] The President's FY2014 budget does not include a table of agency funding for the NRI, but is referred to in the Analytical Perspectives supplement to the President's budget.[31] Also, a brief reference to NSF's participation in the NRI appears in the President's budget for FY2014 as well as multiple references in NSF's FY2014 budget request.[32]

National Network for Manufacturing Innovation

The President's FY2014 budget once again proposes the establishment of a National Network for Manufacturing Innovation (NNMI) to promote the development of manufacturing technologies with broad applications. First proposed in President Obama's FY2013 budget request, this initiative would be carried out through a collaboration among NIST, DOD, DOE, and NSF.[33]

According to NIST, the NNMI would consist of

> a network of institutes where researchers, companies, and entrepreneurs can come together to develop new manufacturing technologies with broad applications. Each institute would have a unique technology focus. These institutes will help support an ecosystem of manufacturing activity in local areas. The Manufacturing Innovation Institutes would support manufacturing technology commercialization by helping to bridge the gap from the laboratory to the market and address core gaps in scaling manufacturing process technologies.[34]

The President's budget requests a mandatory appropriation to NIST of $1 billion over nine years (FY2014-FY2022) in support of up to 15 NNMI manufacturing innovation institutes. Funding for the program would be front-loaded with NIST anticipating obligating $147.6 million in FY2014, and $672 million in spending projected for FY2014-FY2018.[35]

Reorganization of STEM Education Programs

The Administration's FY2014 budget proposes a broad reorganization and consolidation of federal science, technology, engineering, and mathematics (STEM) education programs—including programs with a potential nexus to federal R&D, such as research fellowships at mission agencies. Under the plan, the National Science Foundation, Department of Education, and Smithsonian Institution would become lead federal agencies for graduate/undergraduate

---

[30] Ibid.

[31] Office of Management and Budget, Executive Office of the President, *Analytical Perspectives, Budget of the United States Government, Fiscal Year 2014*, p. 371.

[32] National Science Foundation, *Fiscal Year 2014 Budget of the U.S. Government*, April 10, 2013, http://www.nsf.gov/about/budget/fy2014/pdf/EntireDocument_fy2014.pdf.

[33] Executive Office of the President, Office of Science and Technology Policy, *The 2014 Budget: A World-Leading Commitment to Science and Research—Science, Technology, Innovation, and STEM Education in the 2014 Budget*, April 10, 2013.

[34] U.S. Department of Commerce, *FY2014 Budget in Brief*, February 2012, p. 123, http://www.osec.doc.gov/bmi/budget/FY13BIB/fy2013bib_final.pdf.

[35] Office of Management and Budget, Executive Office of the President, *Fiscal Year 2014 Budget of the U.S. Government*, Supplemental Tables, Table S-9, April 10, 2013, p. 203.

STEM education, kindergarten-through-grade 12 STEM education, and informal science education, respectively.

The President proposes that certain STEM education programs at other federal agencies be reduced and their associated budget authority allocated to the three lead agencies. Other federal STEM education programs, including those at the lead agencies, also would be consolidated under the plan. About half of existing federal STEM education programs would be affected. It is unclear how these proposed changes might affect agency R&D funding levels. The widely anticipated federal STEM education strategy, which Congress directed the Administration to produce, may address some of these questions.[36]

Treatment of FY2013 Rescissions and Sequestration in this Report

Rescissions specified in the Consolidated and Further Continuing Appropriations Act, 2013 (P.L. 113-6), coupled with sequestration requirements in the Budget Control Act of 2011 (BCA, P.L. 112-25) and sequestration process modifications made in the American Taxpayer Relief Act of 2012 (ATRA, P.L. 112-240) have complicated analysis of the level of federal R&D funding provided to federal agencies. The complication is particularly pronounced with respect to accounts, programs, projects, and activities that include both R&D and non-R&D funding as rescissions and sequestration reductions may be applied unequally to the R&D and non-R&D functions. Accordingly, in those cases where the FY2013 R&D funding level cannot be determined with certainty, no figures are provided. FY2013 figures will be added as agencies provide additional information that allows for an accurate determination of R&D funding. Appropriations accounts for some agencies contain only R&D; for most of those agencies, the post-rescission/pre-sequestration funding levels are included. Similarly, for those accounts with both R&D and non-R&D related activities that this report tracks in their entirety, post-rescission/pre-sequestration funding levels are included. The remainder of this section provides background on the acts that require sequestration and the processes to be used in arriving at the amounts to be sequestered, as well as CRS resources that provide additional information.

FY2013 discretionary appropriations were considered in the context of the BCA, which established discretionary spending limits for FY2012-FY2021. The BCA also tasked a Joint Select Committee on Deficit Reduction to develop a federal deficit reduction plan for Congress and the President to enact by January 15, 2012. Because deficit reduction legislation was not enacted by that date, an automatic spending reduction process established by the BCA was triggered; this process consists of a combination of sequestration and lower discretionary spending caps, initially scheduled to begin on January 2, 2013. The "joint committee" sequestration process for FY2013 requires the Office of Management and Budget (OMB) to implement across-the-board spending cuts at the account and program level to achieve equal budget reductions from both defense and nondefense funding at a percentage to be determined, under terms specified in the Balanced Budget and Emergency Deficit Control Act of 1985 (BBEDCA, Title II of P.L. 99-177, 2 U.S.C. 900-922), as amended by the BCA. For further

---

[36] For more information on federal STEM education programs, see CRS Report R42642, *Science, Technology, Engineering, and Mathematics (STEM) Education: A Primer*, by Heather B. Gonzalez and Jeffrey J. Kuenzi.

information on the Budget Control Act, see CRS Report R41965, *The Budget Control Act of 2011*, by Bill Heniff Jr., Elizabeth Rybicki, and Shannon M. Mahan.

The American Taxpayer Relief Act of 2012 (ATRA, P.L. 112-240), enacted on January 2, 2013, made a number of significant changes to the procedures in the BCA that will take place during FY2013. First, the date for the joint committee sequester to be implemented was delayed for two months, until March 1, 2013. Second, the dollar amount of the joint committee sequester was reduced by $24 billion. Third the statutory caps on discretionary spending for FY2013 (and FY2014) were lowered. For further information on the changes to BCA procedures made by ATRA, see CRS Report R42949, *The American Taxpayer Relief Act of 2012: Modifications to the Budget Enforcement Procedures in the Budget Control Act*, by Bill Heniff Jr.

Pursuant to the BCA, as amended by ATRA, President Obama ordered that the joint committee sequester be implemented on March 1, 2013. The accompanying OMB report indicated a dollar amount of budget authority to be canceled to each account containing non-exempt funds. The sequester will ultimately be applied at the program, project, and activity (PPA) level within each account. Because the sequester was implemented at the time that a temporary continuing resolution was in force, the reductions were calculated on an annualized basis and will be apportioned throughout the remainder of the fiscal year. Although full year FY2013 funding has been enacted, the effect of these reductions on the budgetary resources that will ultimately be available to an agency at either the account or PPA level remain unclear until further guidance is provided by OMB as to how these reductions should be applied.

Section 3004 of P.L. 113-6 is intended to eliminate any amount by which the new budget authority provided in the act exceeds the FY2013 discretionary spending limits in Section 251(c)(2) of the Balanced Budget and Emergency Deficit Control Act, as amended by the Budget Control Act of 2011 and the American Taxpayer Relief Act of 2012. As enacted, this section provides two separate across-the-board rescissions—one for non-security budget authority and one for security budget authority—of 0%, to be applied at the program, project, and activity level. The section requires the percentages to be increased if OMB estimates that additional rescissions are needed to avoid exceeding the limits. Subsequent to the enactment of P.L. 113-6, OMB calculated that additional rescissions of 0.032% of security budget authority, and 0.2% of non-security budget authority, would be required.

FY2014 Appropriations Status

The remainder of this report provides a more in-depth analysis of R&D in 12 federal departments and agencies that, in aggregate, receive more than 98% of federal R&D funding. Annual appropriations for these agencies are provided through eight of the 12 regular appropriations bills. For each agency covered in this report, **Table 5** shows the corresponding regular appropriations bill that provides funding for the agency, including its R&D activities.

On October 16, 2013, the House and Senate passed the Continuing Appropriations Act, 2014 (H.R. 2775), which was subsequently signed into law (P.L. 113-46) by President Obama on October 17, 2013. The act provides continuing appropriations for FY2014 generally at the levels of, and under the terms and conditions of, FY2013 funding as reduced by sequestration, until whichever of the following first occurs: (1) enactment of an appropriation for any project or activity provided for in it; (2) enactment of the applicable appropriations Act for FY2014 without any provision for such project or activity; or (3) January 15, 2014.

This report will be updated as relevant appropriations bills are passed by the House or the Senate.

In addition to this report, CRS produces individual reports on each of the appropriations bills. These reports can be accessed via the CRS website at http://crs.gov/Pages/clis.aspx?cliid=73. Also, the status of each appropriations bill is available on the CRS webpage, *Status Table of Appropriations*, available at http://crs.gov/Pages/AppropriationsStatusTable.aspx?source= QuickLinks.

Table 5. Alignment of Agency R&D Funding and Regular Appropriations Bills

Department/Agency	Regular Appropriations Bill
Department of Defense	Department of Defense Appropriations Act
Department of Homeland Security	Department of Homeland Security Appropriations Act
National Institutes of Health	Departments of Labor, Health and Human Services, and Education, and Related Agencies Appropriations Act
Department of Energy	Energy and Water Development and Related Agencies Appropriations Act
National Science Foundation	Commerce, Justice, Science, and Related Agencies Appropriations Act
Department of Commerce - National Institute of Standards and Technology - National Oceanic and Atmospheric Administration	Commerce, Justice, Science, and Related Agencies Appropriations Act
National Aeronautics and Space Administration	Commerce, Justice, Science, and Related Agencies Appropriations Act
Department of Agriculture	Agriculture, Rural Development, Food and Drug Administration, and Related Agencies Appropriations Act
Department of the Interior	Department of the Interior, Environment, and Related Agencies Appropriations Act
Environmental Protection Agency	Department of the Interior, Environment, and Related Agencies Appropriations Act
Department of Transportation	Transportation, Housing and Urban Development, and Related Agencies Appropriations Act

Source: CRS website, FY2014 Status Table of Appropriations, available at http://crs.gov/Pages/ AppropriationsStatusTable.aspx?source=QuickLinks.

Department of Defense[37]

Congress supports research and development in the Department of Defense (DOD) primarily through its Research, Development, Test, and Evaluation (RDT&E) appropriation. The appropriation supports the development of the nation's future military hardware and software and the technology base upon which those products rely.

Nearly all of what DOD spends on RDT&E is appropriated in Title IV of the defense appropriation bill. (See **Table 6**.) However, RDT&E funds are also appropriated in other parts of

---

[37] This section was written by John Moteff, Specialist in Science and Technology Policy, CRS Resources, Science, and Industry Division.

the bill. For example, RDT&E funds are appropriated as part of the Defense Health Program, the Chemical Agents and Munitions Destruction Program, and the National Defense Sealift Fund. The Defense Health Program supports the delivery of health care to DOD personnel and their families. Program funds are requested through the Operations and Maintenance appropriations request. The program's RDT&E funds support congressionally directed research in such areas as breast, prostate, and ovarian cancer and other medical conditions. Congress appropriates funds for this program in Title VI (Other Department of Defense Programs) of the defense appropriations bill. The Chemical Agents and Munitions Destruction Program supports activities to destroy the U.S. inventory of lethal chemical agents and munitions to avoid future risks and costs associated with storage. Funds for this program are requested through the Defensewide Procurement appropriations request. Congress appropriates funds for this program also in Title VI. The National Defense Sealift Fund supports the procurement, operation and maintenance, and research and development of the nation's naval reserve fleet and supports a U.S. flagged merchant fleet that can serve in time of need. Requests for this fund are made as part of the Navy's Operations and Maintenance appropriation request. Congress appropriates funds for this program in Title V (Revolving and Management Funds) of the defense appropriations bill.

The Joint Improvised Explosive Device Defeat Fund (JIEDDF) also contains RDT&E monies. However, the fund does not contain an RDT&E line item as do the three programs mentioned above. The Joint Improvised Explosive Device Defeat Office, which administers the fund, tracks (but does not report) the amount of funding allocated to RDT&E. The JIEDDF funding is not included in the table below.

RDT&E funds also have been requested and appropriated as part of DOD's separate funding to support efforts in what the Bush Administration had termed the Global War on Terror (GWOT), and what the Obama Administration refers to as Overseas Contingency Operations (OCO). Typically, the RDT&E funds appropriated for GWOT/OCO activities go to specified Program Elements (PEs) in Title IV. However, they are requested and accounted for separately. The Bush Administration requested these funds in separate GWOT emergency supplemental requests. The Obama Administration, while continuing to identify these funds uniquely as OCO requests, has included these funds as part of the regular budget, not in emergency supplementals. However, the Obama Administration has asked for additional OCO funds in supplemental requests, if the initial OCO funding is not enough to get through the fiscal year.

In addition, GWOT/OCO-related requests/appropriations often include money for a number of transfer funds. These have included in the past the Iraqi Freedom Fund (IFF), the Iraqi Security Forces Fund, the Afghanistan Security Forces Fund, and the Pakistan Counterinsurgency Capability Fund. Another transfer fund is the Mine Resistant and Ambush Protected Vehicle Fund (MRAPVF). Congress typically makes a single appropriation into each of these funds, and authorizes the Secretary to make transfers to other accounts, including RDT&E, at his discretion.

For FY2014, the Obama Administration requested $67.520 billion for DOD's baseline Title IV RDT&E. This is $5.449 billion less than what was available in FY2012 for both baseline and OCO RDT&E. It is $2.339 billion less than what was provided for baseline FY2013 RDT&E funding in the Consolidated and Continuing Appropriations Act (H.R. 933). However, this does not consider the subsequent sequestration. According to the Department's FY2014 Budget Briefing Documents, sequestration reduced the FY2013 RDT&E funding to $63.400 billion. Therefore, the FY2014 request would be $4.120 billion above the FY2013 sequestered balance. The Administration also requested $117 million in OCO RDT&E, approximately half of what was appropriated for OCO RDT&E in FY2013. The FY2014 OCO RDT&E request was directed almost exclusively toward classified programs.

In addition to the baseline Title IV RDT&E request, the Administration requested $684 million in RDT&E through the Defense Health Program, $613 million in RDT&E through the Chemical Agents and Munitions Destruction program, and $56 million in RDT&E through the National Defense Sealift Fund for FY2014.

The House approved its version of the DOD appropriations bill (H.R. 2397) on July 24. The House provided $66.399 billion for Title IV RDT&E, $1.121 billion less than what was requested. It also approved $117 million for OCO RDT&E, as requested. Reductions in the baseline program were often associated with program delays or program increases which the House considered to be unjustified. Two relatively large increases were $250 million for the Office of the Secretary to help administer the Rapid Innovation Fund and $173 million for missile defense programs within the Israeli Cooperative Programs line item. The House also approved $56 million in RDT&E for the National Defense Sealift Fund (as requested) and $604 million in RDT&E for the Chemical Agents and Munitions Destruction Program ($9 million below the request). The House approved $1.356 billion in RDT&E for the Defense Health Program (nearly doubling the request), which includes an additional $20.5 million added on the floor of the House.

The Senate Appropriations Committee reported its version of the DOD appropriations bill (S. 1429) on August 1. The Committee recommended $65.807 billion in baseline Title IV RDT&E, a little under $600 million below the House approved figure. Relatively large increases were an additional $173 million for the Israeli Cooperative Program, with the increase focused on missile defense technology, and $150 million for the Rapid Innovation Program. Relatively large reductions included $106 million in the Army's Warfighter Information Network, $143 million in the Missile Defense Agency's Midcourse Defense Segment (with those funds transferred to the agency's operations and maintenance account), $169 million in the Army's Manned Ground Vehicles program, and $192 million in the Air Force's CSAR HH-130 recapitalization program. Except for the missile defense midcourse program, reductions were attributed to restoring acquisition accountability. The Senate Appropriations Committee also recommended $56 million for the National Defense Sealift Fund (as requested), $604 million for the Chemical Agents and Munitions Destruction program (as requested), and $1.319 billion for RDT&E in the Defense Health Program. The Senate Appropriations Committee provided $89 million in OCO-related RDT&E, providing none of the requested funds for Navy OCO-related funding, but increasing the Army's OCO RDT&E request by $7 million.

RDT&E funding can be analyzed in different ways. Each of the military departments request and receive their own RDT&E funding. So, too, do various DOD agencies (e.g., the Missile Defense Agency and the Defense Advanced Research Projects Agency), collectively aggregated within the Defensewide account. RDT&E funding also can be characterized by budget activity (i.e., the type of RDT&E supported). Those budget activities designated as 6.1, 6.2, and 6.3 (basic research, applied research, and advanced technology development, respectively) constitute what is called DOD's Science and Technology Program (S&T) and represent the more research-oriented part of the RDT&E program. Budget activities 6.4 and 6.5 focus on the development of specific weapon systems or components (e.g., the Joint Strike Fighter or missile defense systems), for which an operational need has been determined and an acquisition program established. Budget activity 6.6 provides management support, including support for test and evaluation facilities. Budget activity 6.7 supports system improvements in existing operational systems.

Many congressional policymakers are particularly interested in S&T funding since these funds support the development of new technologies and the underlying science. Some in the defense community see ensuring adequate support for S&T activities as imperative to maintaining U.S. military superiority. The knowledge generated at this stage of development can also contribute to advances in commercial technologies.

The FY2014 Title IV baseline S&T funding request was $11.984 billion, $0.074 billion below what was available for S&T in FY2012. According to its FY2014 Budget Request Overview, the FY2014 S&T budget request emphasizes activities aligned with the Department's recent shift in strategic focus from Iraq and Afghanistan to the Asia-Pacific region. This is reflected in funding for technologies aimed at defeating anti-access/area denial capabilities of potential adversaries, counter weapons of mass destruction, efficient operations in cyberspace and space, electronic warfare, and high-speed kinetic strike capability.

The House approved $12.317 billion in Title IV baseline S&T funding, $333 million more than what was requested. Each of the three S&T-related budget activities in all the accounts was increased above the requested level. The Senate Appropriations Committee recommended $12.050 million in Title IV baseline S&T funding.

Within the S&T program, basic research (6.1) receives special attention, particularly by the nation's universities. DOD is not a large supporter of basic research, when compared to NIH or NSF. However, over half of DOD's basic research budget is spent at universities and represents the major contribution of funds in some areas of science and technology (such as electrical engineering and material science). The Administration requested $2.165 billion for basic research for FY2014.

The House approved $2.170 billion in basic research, roughly what was requested. The increase of $5 million went to the Historically Black Colleges and Universities line item in the Defensewide account. The Senate Appropriations Committee also recommended $2.170 billion in basic research. However, it increased the Navy's Defense Research Science program by $5 million.

Table 6. Department of Defense RDT&E

(in millions of dollars)

Budget Account	FY2012 Actual Base + OCO	FY2013 Enacted[a] Base	OCO	FY2014 Request Base	OCO	FY2014 House Base	OCO	FY2014 Senate Base	OCO
Army	8,705	8,668	30	7,989	7	7,961	7	7,576	14
Navy	17,723	16,946	53	15,975	34	15,368	34	15,403	
Air Force	26,631	25,407	53	25,703	9	24,947	9	24,946	9
Defensewide	19,722	18,613	112	17,667	66	17,876[a]	66	17,695	66
Dir. Test & Eval.	188	224		186		247		186	
Total Title IV—By Account[c]	**72,970**	**69,859**	**248**	**67,520**	**117**	**66,399**	**117**	**65,807**	**89**

Budget Account	FY2012 Actual Base + OCO	FY2013 Enacted[a] Base	FY2013 Enacted[a] OCO	FY2014 Request Base	FY2014 Request OCO	FY2014 House Base	FY2014 House OCO	FY2014 Senate Base	FY2014 Senate OCO
Budget Activity									
6.1 Basic Research	2,010	2,128		2,165		2,170		2,170	
6.2 Applied Research	4,730	4,720		4,627		4,679		4,642	
6.3 Advanced Dev.	5,318	5,623		5,192		5,467		5,238	
6.4 Advanced Component Dev. and Prototypes	13,579	12,635	19	12,057		11,775		11,908	7
6.5 Systems Dev. And Demo	13,573	13,990	17	13,699	7	13,046	7	12,611	7
6.6 Management Support[d]	5,694	4,515	5	4,325		4,166		4,370	
6.7 Op. Systems Dev.[e]	28,065	26,247	206	25,456	110	25,106	110	24,868	75
Total Title IV—by Budget Activity[c]	**72,970**	**69,859**	**247**	**67,520**	**117**	**6,410[a]**	**117**	**65,807**	**89**
Title V—Revolving and Management Funds									
National Defense Sealift Fund	51	37		56		56		56	
Title VI—Other Defense Programs									
Office of Inspector General	0			0					
Defense Health Program	1,274	1,307		684		1,356[g]		1,319	
Chemical Agents and Munitions Destruction	411	647		613		604		604	
Grand Total[h]	**74,706**	**71,850**	**247**	**68,873**		**68,415[a]**	**117**	**67,786**	**89**

Source: CRS, adapted from the Department of Defense Budget, Fiscal Year 2014 RDT&E Programs (R-1), April 2013, relevant FY2014 Budget Justification (R-2) documents, H.R. 933, H.R. 2397, H.Rept. 113-113, S. 1429, and S.Rept. 113-85.

a. Includes rescission of 0.1% pursuant to Sec. 3001, Div. G of H.R. 933, but not sequester.

b. Includes $10 million reduction made on the House floor to offset a $10 million increase in prostate cancer research in the Defense Health Program.

c. Total may differ from sum of components due to rounding.

d. Includes funding for the Director of Test and Evaluation.

e. Includes funding for classified programs.

f. Does not include the $10 million reduction to Defensewide RDT&E made on the House floor.

g. Includes $20.5 million added on the House floor for prostate cancer, breast cancer, and post-traumatic stress research.

h. The "Grand Total" figure uses the "Total Title IV—by Account" figure.

i.   Does include the $10 million reduction made to the Defensewide RDT&E account on the House floor.

Department of Homeland Security[38]

The President has requested $1.838 billion for R&D and related programs in the Department of Homeland Security (DHS) in FY2014. This is a 64% increase from $1.123 billion in FY2013.[39] The total includes $1.527 billion for the Directorate of Science and Technology (S&T), $291 million for the Domestic Nuclear Detection Office (DNDO), and $20 million for Research, Development, Test, and Evaluation (RDT&E) in the U.S. Coast Guard. The House-passed bill would provide $1.225 billion for S&T, $291 million for DNDO, and $10 million for Coast Guard RDT&E. The Senate-reported bill would provide $1.218 billion for S&T, $289 million for DNDO, and $20 million for Coast Guard RST&E. (See **Table 7**.)

The S&T Directorate is the primary DHS R&D organization.[40] Led by the Under Secretary for Science and Technology, the S&T Directorate performs R&D in several laboratories of its own and funds R&D performed by the DOE national laboratories, industry, universities, and others. The Administration has requested $1.527 billion for the S&T Directorate for FY2014. This is 91% more than the FY2013 operating plan level of $801 million. The increase results largely from the request for $714 million in Laboratory Facilities for construction of the National Bio and Agro-Defense Facility (NBAF). The NBAF is a planned replacement for the current Plum Island Animal Disease Center. According to DHS, the FY2014 request (together with anticipated gift funds from the state of Kansas) would be sufficient to fully fund NBAF construction, which DHS expects to complete in FY2020. The total estimated cost of the NBAF project, including the Kansas contribution and federal funds already appropriated, is $1.230 billion. The previous estimate in the FY2012 budget was $725 million.[41] In University Programs, the requested $31 million in FY2014 is a decrease of 19% from $38 million in the FY2013 operating plan. This decrease reflects a reduction in funding for university centers of excellence and the elimination of funding for scholarships and fellowships. The latter is part of a government-wide consolidation of STEM education activities, discussed earlier in the "Reorganization of STEM Education Programs" section of this report. According to DHS, it will work with the National Science Foundation to ensure that consolidated STEM education activities align with DHS needs.

The House bill would provide $1.225 billion for S&T. This total includes $404 million for NBAF construction, the amount needed to "fully leverage funding contributions by the State of Kansas" (i.e., to provide the 2-to-1 federal matching funds required for $202 million in state bonds). The House provision of $40 million for University Programs would increase funding for university

---

[38] This section was written by Daniel Morgan, Specialist in Science and Technology Policy, CRS Resources, Science, and Industry Division.

[39] FY2013 amounts in this section are from Department of Homeland Security, Office of the Chief Financial Officer, *U.S. Department of Homeland Security Fiscal Year 2013 Post-Sequestration Operating Plan*, April 26, 2013. They do not include funding appropriated by the Disaster Relief Appropriations Act, 2013 (P.L. 113-2). That act appropriated approximately $3 million for the S&T Directorate and approximately $4 million for DNDO.

[40] For more information, see CRS Report R43064, *The DHS S&T Directorate: Selected Issues for Congress*, by Dana A. Shea.

[41] Department of Homeland Security, *Congressional Budget Justification: FY2012*, "Science and Technology Directorate: Research, Development, Acquisitions, and Operations," p. 134. The FY2013 budget did not present a cost estimate for NBAF. At the time the FY2013 budget was released, DHS was reassessing whether to go forward with the NBAF project.

---

centers of excellence; the House report did not address the proposed elimination of scholarship and fellowship funding in University Programs.

The Senate bill would provide $1.218 billion for S&T. Like the House bill, it includes $404 million for NBAF, sufficient to "fully leverage" state contributions. The Senate recommendation of $33 million for University Programs "recognizes the requested reduction ... resulting from the consolidation of the Scholars and Fellows program within the National Science Foundation."

The Domestic Nuclear Detection Office is the DHS organization responsible for nuclear detection research, development, testing, evaluation, acquisition, and operational support. The Administration has requested $291 million for DNDO for FY2014, a decrease of 4% from $303 million in the FY2013 operating plan. In the Research, Development, and Operations account, funding for Systems Architecture and Systems Development would decrease relative to FY2013, while funding for Transformational R&D and Assessments would increase. These shifts appear to reflect DNDO's ongoing transition from large-scale, government-sponsored technology development initiatives to a commercial-first approach to technology acquisition. In the Systems Acquisition account, the request of $14 million for Human Portable Radiation Detection Systems (HPRDS) is a 50% decrease from $27 million in FY2013. The DHS budget justification for HPRDS, however, describes the request as an increase relative to the $8 million the program received under the FY2013 continuing resolution. It is unclear how the higher amount the program received in the FY2013 operating plan will affect the program's plans for FY2014. The House bill would provide the requested amount for DNDO. The Senate bill would provide $289 million, with small reductions in the Management and Administration account and each of the six elements of the Research, Development, and Operations account.

In September 2012, the Government Accountability Office (GAO) reported that although the S&T Directorate, DNDO, and the Coast Guard are the only DHS components that report R&D activities to the Office of Management and Budget, several other DHS components also fund R&D and activities related to R&D.[42] The GAO report found that DHS lacks department-wide policies to define R&D and guide reporting of R&D activities, and as a result, DHS does not know the total amount its components invest in R&D. The report recommended that DHS develop policies and guidance for defining, reporting, and coordinating R&D activities across the department, and that DHS establish a mechanism to track R&D projects. In March 2013, the explanatory statement for the Consolidated and Further Continuing Appropriations Act, 2013 (P.L. 113-6) directed the Secretary of Homeland Security, through the Under Secretary for Science and Technology, to establish a review process for all R&D and related work within DHS.[43] In April 2013, citing its September 2012 report, GAO listed DHS R&D as an area of concern in its annual report on fragmented, overlapping, or duplicative federal programs.[44] The House bill would direct DHS to submit a report on reforms to its R&D programs, including a formal process for setting R&D priorities, a formal process for DHS-wide involvement in R&D decision-making and review, metrics for R&D program status and return on investment, and the implementation of GAO's recommendations. The Senate bill language includes no provision on this topic, but report language directs DHS to implement policies and guidance for defining and

---

[42] Government Accountability Office, *Department of Homeland Security: Oversight and Coordination of Research and Development Should Be Strengthened*, GAO-12-837, Sep 12, 2012.

[43] *Congressional Record*, March 11, 2013, p. S1547.

[44] Government Accountability Office, *2013 Annual Report: Actions Needed to Reduce Fragmentation, Overlap, and Duplication and Achieve Other Financial Benefits*, GAO-13-279SP, April 2013.

overseeing R&D, in accordance with the GAO recommendations. The Senate report also directs DHS to "expeditiously continue" the implementation of R&D portfolio reviews in additional DHS components "to improve the coordinated approach to R&D and related activities within DHS."

Table 7. Department of Homeland Security R&D and Related Programs

(budget authority in millions of dollars)

	FY2012 Actual	FY2013 Op. Plan	FY2014 Request	FY2014 House	FY2014 Sen. Cte.
Directorate of Science and Technology	**$673**	**$801**	**$1,527**	**$1,225**	**$1,218**
Management and Administration	135	127	130	129	129
R&D, Acquisition, and Operations	538	674	1,397	1,096	1,089
Research, Development, and Innovation	*266*	*432*	*467*	*467*	*467*
Laboratory Facilities	*182*	*158*	*858*	*548*	*548*
Acquisition and Operations Support	*54*	*46*	*42*	*42*	*42*
University Programs	*37*	*38*	*31*	*40*	*33*
Domestic Nuclear Detection Office	**290**	**303**	**291**	**291**	**289**
Management and Administration	38	38	38	37	37
Research, Development, and Operations	215	216	211	211	209
Systems Architecture	*30*	*29*	*21*	*21*	*21*
Systems Development	*51*	*27*	*21*	*21*	*21*
Transformational R&D	*40*	*71*	*75*	*75*	*75*
Assessments	*38*	*31*	*40*	*40*	*39*
Operations Support	*33*	*34*	*31*	*31*	*30*
National Technical Nuclear Forensics Center	*23*	*24*	*23*	*23*	*23*
Systems Acquisition	37	50	43	43	43
Radiation Portal Monitors Program	*2*	*1*	*7*	*7*	*7*
Securing the Cities	*22*	*21*	*22*	*22*	*22*
Human Portable Radiation Detection Systems	*14*	*27*	*14*	*14*	*14*
U.S. Coast Guard RDT&E	**28**	**20**	**20**	**10**	**20**
TOTAL	**991**	**1,123**	**1,838**	**1,527**	**1,527**

Sources: FY2012 actual and FY2014 request from DHS FY2014 congressional budget justification, http://www.dhs.gov/xabout/budget/dhs-budget.shtm. FY2013 operating plan from Department of Homeland Security, Office of the Chief Financial Officer, *U.S. Department of Homeland Security Fiscal Year 2013 Post-Sequestration Operating Plan*, April 26, 2013. FY2014 House from H.R. 2217 as passed by the House and H.Rept. 113-91. FY2014 Senate Committee from H.R. 2217 as reported in the Senate and S.Rept. 113-77.

Notes: FY2013 operating plan amounts do not include approximately $7 million appropriated by the Disaster Relief Appropriations Act, 2013 (P.L. 113-2). Totals may differ from sum of components due to rounding.

National Institutes of Health[45]

The FY2014 President's Budget requests a program level total of $31.331 billion for NIH, an increase of $2.180 billion (7.5%) over the FY2013 post-sequester operating plan level of $29.151 billion, and $471 million (1.5%) more than the comparable FY2012 amount of $30.860 billion (see **Table 8**). The request would give most of the institutes and centers roughly proportional increases, while a few specific activities are proposed for larger increases that account for most of the additional funding.

On July 11, 2013, the Senate Appropriations Committee reported S. 1284 (S.Rept. 113-71), its FY2014 bill for the Departments of Labor, Health and Human Services, and Education, and Related Agencies (Labor/HHS). The committee-recommended program level funding for NIH would be $31.184 billion, $147 million (0.5%) lower than the President's request, $2.033 billion (7.0%) over the FY2013 operating plan, and $324 million (1.0%) more than FY2012. The committee report, after explaining the $147 million cut compared to the Administration's request (see below), characterized the total for NIH as "effectively equal to the budget request." The House has not yet taken action on an FY2014 Labor/HHS bill. Currently, federal agencies are operating under the provisions of P.L. 113-46, the Continuing Appropriations Act, 2014 (H.R. 2775), which was signed into law by President Obama on October 17, 2013. The act provides continuing appropriations for FY2014 until January 15, 2014, generally at FY2013 post-sequestration levels, unless regular appropriations are enacted sooner.

In this discussion, FY2014 requested and committee-recommended amounts for NIH programs are compared to either FY2012 actual levels or FY2013 operating plan levels, or both, depending on information available. FY2013 amounts cited in the Senate committee report are not operating plan levels and are not discussed here.[46]

NIH Organization and Sources of Funding. NIH supports and conducts a wide range of basic and clinical research, research training, and health information dissemination across all fields of biomedical and behavioral sciences. About 83% of NIH's budget goes out to the extramural research community in the form of grants, contracts, and other awards. The funding supports research performed by more than 300,000 non-federal scientists and technical personnel who work at more than 2,500 universities, hospitals, medical schools, and other research institutions around the country and abroad.[47] The agency's organization consists of the Office of the NIH Director and 27 institutes and centers. The Office of the Director (OD) sets overall policy for NIH and coordinates the programs and activities of all NIH components, particularly in areas of research that involve multiple institutes. The institutes and centers (collectively called ICs) focus on particular diseases, areas of human health and development, or aspects of research support. Each IC plans and manages its own research programs in coordination with the Office of the Director. As shown in **Table 8**, Congress provides a separate appropriation to 24 of the 27 ICs, to

---

[45] This section was written by Pamela W. Smith, Analyst in Biomedical Policy, CRS Domestic Social Policy Division. For background information on NIH, see CRS Report R41705, *The National Institutes of Health (NIH): Organization, Funding, and Congressional Issues*, by Judith A. Johnson and Pamela W. Smith.

[46] Senate committee amounts reflect funding enacted under P.L. 113-6, the Consolidated and Further Continuing Appropriations Act, 2013 (including across-the-board rescissions), but do not reflect the March 1, 2013, sequestration or additional administrative transfers.

[47] U.S. Department of Health and Human Services, *FY2014 Budget in Brief*, April 10, 2013, p. 34, http://www.hhs.gov/budget/fy2014/fy-2014-budget-in-brief.pdf.

OD, and to an intramural Buildings and Facilities account. (The other three centers, which perform centralized support services, are funded through assessments on the IC appropriations.)

Funding for NIH comes primarily from the annual Labor/HHS appropriations bill, with an additional amount for Superfund-related activities from the appropriations bill for the Department of the Interior, Environment, and Related Agencies (Interior/Environment). Those two bills provide NIH's discretionary budget authority. In addition, NIH receives mandatory funding of $150 million annually that is provided in the Public Health Service (PHS) Act for a special program on type 1 diabetes research, and also receives $8.2 million annually for the National Library of Medicine from a transfer within PHS. The total funding available for NIH activities, taking account of add-ons and transfers, is the program level.

Except for the mandatory diabetes funding, Congress does not usually specify amounts for particular diseases or research areas. Similarly, NIH does not expressly budget by disease category.[48] Some bills may propose authorizations for designated research purposes, but funding would generally remain subject to the discretionary appropriations process.

NIH and other HHS agencies and programs that are authorized under the PHS Act are subject to a budget assessment called the PHS Program Evaluation Set-Aside, also called the evaluation tap. Section 241 of the PHS Act (42 U.S.C. §238j) authorizes the Secretary to use a portion of eligible appropriations to study the effectiveness of federal health programs and to identify ways to improve them. Congress sets the percentage level of the tap in the annual Labor/HHS appropriations acts, and also directs specific amounts of funding from the tap for transfer to a number of HHS programs. The set-aside has the effect of redistributing appropriated funds for specific purposes among PHS and other HHS agencies. NIH, with the largest budget among the PHS agencies, becomes the largest "donor" of program evaluation funds, and is a relatively minor recipient. Section 205 of the FY2012 Labor/HHS appropriations act capped the set-aside at 2.5%, which drew over $700 million from the NIH budget. The same amount was assessed in FY2013 under the continuing appropriations act. The FY2014 President's Budget proposes to increase the PHS set-aside to 3.0%; the Senate committee rejected the increase, largely because of its effect on NIH. The committee estimated that the increased assessment would have taken an extra $147 million from NIH.[49] By convention, budget tables such as **Table 8** do not subtract the amount of the evaluation tap from the agencies' appropriations.[50]

FY2014 President's Budget Request and Senate Committee Recommendation. In the request, most of the institutes and centers would receive increases of about 1% compared to FY2012 and about 7% compared to the FY2013 operating level, with selected exceptions reflecting program priorities. The Senate committee largely supported the Administration's priorities, with a few variations. NIH describes its areas of emphasis for FY2014 under four broad themes that build on its current activities, provide for some new initiatives, and continue the implementation of an organizational restructuring for translational medicine that started in FY2012.

---

[48] See NIH website, "Estimates of Funding for Various Research, Condition, and Disease Categories (RCDC)," http://report.nih.gov/categorical_spending.aspx.

[49] See S.Rept. 113-71 on S. 1284, p. 41 and p. 83.

[50] For further information on the PHS Evaluation Set-Aside, see CRS Report R41737, *Public Health Service (PHS) Agencies: Overview and Funding, FY2010-FY2012*, coordinated by C. Stephen Redhead and Pamela W. Smith.

Theme 1: Investing in Basic Research. About 53% of the proposed budget would be spent on basic research to understand the causes of disease onset and progression. In neurosciences, about $40 million is requested for the new multi-agency Brain Research through Application of Innovative Neurotechnologies (BRAIN) initiative to develop tools for the study of complex brain functions. The Senate committee supported that amount as an initial investment. To improve the handling, sharing, and analysis of large digital datasets of information, $41 million is requested for a new program called Big Data to Knowledge (BD2K) through the NIH Common Fund.

Theme 2: Advancing Translational Sciences. Translational medicine, a function of all the ICs, focuses on converting basic research discoveries into clinical applications that benefit patients. In the FY2012 appropriations act, Congress approved an NIH reorganization that consolidated various resource programs into a new National Center for Advancing Translational Sciences (NCATS). NCATS explores improved methods to test possible new therapies and encourage their commercialization and dissemination. The FY2014 request for NCATS is $666 million, an increase of $91 million (16%) over its FY2012 first-year budget. The Senate committee approved $661 million, a 15% increase over FY2012 and $119 million (22%) above the FY2013 operating plan level. Over $40 million of the increase would go to expanding the Cures Acceleration Network (CAN) from $10 million at its start in FY2012 to $50 million in FY2014.

Theme 3: Recruiting and Retaining Diverse Scientific Talent and Creativity for the Research Workforce. NIH analysis of the biomedical workforce and future training needs has led to a special focus on promoting diversity and understanding barriers to career advancement. NIH is implementing new measures, supported by the Senate committee, to assist trainees and track their career progress. The request includes $32 million for a new Workforce Diversity Initiative being piloted through the NIH Common Fund. It will support a consortium of under-resourced institutions and create a National Research Mentoring Network. NIH requests $776 million for its major research training program, the Ruth L. Kirschstein National Research Service Awards, with stipend increases for trainees. The request is $14 million (2%) above the FY2012 level and $39 million (5%) above the FY2013 operating plan.

Theme 4: Restoring American Competitiveness. The NIH budget summary offers economic arguments for support of health research.[51] It cites studies of the impact of health research on, for example, reductions in death rates and increased life expectancy, as well as studies linking NIH funding to direct and indirect support of U.S. jobs and to growth of private investment in life sciences research. The summary discusses global competition in the sciences, especially Asian and European R&D efforts, and warns of erosion in the U.S. leadership position, an observation echoed in the committee report.

The following are selected other program changes and areas of emphasis in NIH accounts.

Alzheimer's disease research: To continue implementing the research components of the National Plan to Address Alzheimer's Disease (AD), NIH estimates it will spend $562 million on AD research in FY2014, up $59 million (12%) from FY2012. The total budget request for the National Institute on Aging (NIA), at 7% above FY2012, includes an increase of $80 million

---

[51] U.S. Department of Health and Human Services, National Institutes of Health, *FY2014 Justification of Estimates for Appropriations Committees*, Vol. I - Overview/Executive Summary, April 10, 2013, pp. ES-24-28, http://officeofbudget.od nih.gov/pdfs/FY14/Tab%201%20-%20Executive%20Summary_final.pdf.

(24%) for research on AD. The committee recommended a 6% increase for NIA over FY2012 (14% over the FY2013 operating plan), but declined to specify an amount for AD research.

Institutional Development Awards (IDeA): The IDeA program, housed in the National Institute of General Medical Sciences, supports research capacity and infrastructure grants at institutions in states that have historically received less NIH research support. For FY2014, NIH requests $225 million for IDeA, reversing an increase Congress gave the program in FY2012. The committee rejected the proposed cut and recommended restoring the FY2012 level of $276 million, commenting also that the eligibility criteria for the grants should be revisited.

Science, Technology, Engineering, and Mathematics (STEM) education: As part of a proposed government-wide reorganization of STEM education (see "Reorganization of STEM Education Programs"), the Administration planned to eliminate or consolidate nine NIH STEM programs totaling $26 million, including a $15.4 million reduction in the Science Education Partnership Awards program in OD. The committee directed NIH to continue funding the programs.

Office of the Director/Common Fund: The FY2014 request for OD includes new funding for the Common Fund and for strategic initiatives, such as $31 million for a new Biomedical Innovation Opportunities-Fund (BIO-F) to facilitate a rapid response to new ideas and unexpected scientific opportunities. The Common Fund supports research in emerging areas of scientific opportunity, public health challenges, or knowledge gaps that might benefit from collaboration between two or more institutes or centers. The request for the Common Fund is $573 million, $28 million (5%) higher than the FY2012 level, including funding for the new BD2K program. The committee recommended $568 million for the Common Fund and did not comment on the BIO-F proposal.

Research Project Grants: The main funding mechanism for supporting extramural research is research project grants (RPGs), which are competitive, peer-reviewed, and largely investigator-initiated. The FY2014 budget requests total funding for RPGs of $16.9 billion, representing about 54% of NIH's proposed budget. The amount is an increase of $382 million (2%) over the FY2012 level and $1.384 billion (9%) over the FY2013 operating plan. The request would support an estimated 36,610 RPG awards, 351 more grants than in FY2012 and 1,708 more grants than in FY2013. Within that total, 10,269 would be competing RPGs, 1,283 (14%) more than in FY2012 and 1,986 (24%) more than in FY2013. ("Competing" awards means new grants plus competing renewals of existing grants.) The average cost of a competing RPG in FY2014 is estimated to be about $456,000, up from about $421,000 in FY2012. The increase is mainly due to the cycling of high-cost HIV/AIDS Clinical Trials Networks grants into competing status in FY2014. After adjusting for those large grants, the average cost of competing RPGs is estimated to be about $420,000, or approximately the same as in FY2012. To maximize the number of new and competing grants in FY2014, NIH proposes to continue the FY2012 grant awards policy of eliminating inflation increases for future year commitments for all competing and non-competing awards.[52] Adjustments for special needs, however, such as equipment and added personnel, would continue to be accommodated. The Senate committee did not comment on specific funding mechanisms or grants policies.

---

[52] National Institutes of Health, *NIH Fiscal Policy for Grant Awards - FY2012*, Notice NOT-OD-12-036, January 20, 2012, http://grants nih.gov/grants/guide/notice-files/NOT-OD-12-036 html. See also the NIH Extramural Financial Operations website at http://grants.nih.gov/grants/financial/index.htm for yearly plans and resources.

Other Funding Mechanisms: In the Administration's request, support for *research centers*, at $2.846 billion (includes IDeA centers), would be $195 million (6%) below FY2012 and $97 million (4%) above FY2013. The catch-all *R&D contracts* mechanism would increase by $93 million (3%) over FY2012 and by $277 million (10%) over FY2013 to $3.030 billion (includes the proposed increase in the PHS evaluation tap, which the committee rejected). The NIH *intramural research program* would gain $94 million (3%) over FY2012 and $234 million (7%) over FY2013 for a total of $3.503 billion. *Research management and support* would increase by $19 million (1%) compared to FY2012 and $67 million (5%) over FY2013 to $1.550 billion. The *Buildings and Facilities* mechanism, at $134 million, would be $1 million (1%) more than FY2012 and $8 million (7%) more than FY2013.

Table 8. National Institutes of Health Funding

(in millions of dollars)

National Institutes/National Centers; Other Components	FY2012 Actual[a]	FY2013 Operating Plan[b]	FY2014 Request	FY2014 Senate Committee
National Cancer Institute (NCI)	5,063	4,779	5,126	5,092
National Heart, Lung, & Blood Institute (NHLBI)	3,073	2,901	3,099	3,078
Dental/Craniofacial Research (NIDCR)	410	387	412	410
Diabetes/Digestive/Kidney (NIDDK)[c]	1,794	1,693	1,812	1,800
Neurological Disorders/Stroke (NINDS)	1,623	1,532	1,643	1,632
Allergy/Infectious Diseases (NIAID)[d]	4,482	4,231	4,579	4,548
General Medical Sciences (NIGMS)	2,426	2,291	2,401	2,436
Child Health/Human Development (NICHD)	1,319	1,245	1,339	1,330
National Eye Institute (NEI)	701	662	699	701
Environmental Health Sciences (NIEHS)	684	646	691	687
National Institute on Aging (NIA)	1,120	1,040	1,193	1,185
Arthritis/Musculoskeletal/Skin Diseases (NIAMS)	535	505	541	537
Deafness/Communication Disorders (NIDCD)	416	392	423	420
National Institute of Nursing Research (NINR)	145	136	146	145
Alcohol Abuse/Alcoholism (NIAAA)	459	433	464	461
National Institute on Drug Abuse (NIDA)	1,051	993	1,072	1,064
National Institute of Mental Health (NIMH)[d]	1,478	1,395	1,466	1,456
Nat'l Human Genome Research Inst (NHGRI)	512	483	517	514
Biomedical Imaging/Bioengineering (NIBIB)	338	319	339	338
Complementary/Alternative Medicine (NCCAM)	128	121	129	128
Minority Health/Health Disparities (NIMHD)	276	260	283	281
Fogarty International Center (FIC)	69	66	73	72
Advancing Translational Sciences (NCATS)	574	542	666	661
National Library of Medicine (NLM)	365	318	382	380
Office of Director (OD)	1,457	1,436	1,473	1,464

National Institutes/National Centers; Other Components	FY2012 Actual[a]	FY2013 Operating Plan[b]	FY2014 Request	FY2014 Senate Committee
Buildings & Facilities (B&F)	125	118	126	125
Subtotal, Labor/HHS Appropriation	**30,623**	**28,926**	**31,094**	**30,947**
Superfund (Interior appropriation to NIEHS)[e]	79	75	79	79
Total, NIH discretionary budget authority	**30,702**	**29,001**	**31,173**	**31,026**
Pre-appropriated type 1 diabetes funds[f]	150	142	150	150
PHS Evaluation Tap funding[g]	8	8	8	8
Total, NIH program level	**30,860**	**29,151**	**31,331**	**31,184**

Sources: FY2012 Actual and FY2014 Request are adapted by CRS from National Institutes of Health, *Justification of Estimates for Appropriations Committees, FY2014,* Vol. I—Overview/Supplementary Tables, April 10, 2013, p. ST-2, http://officeofbudget.od.nih.gov/pdfs/FY14/FY%202014_Supplementary%20Tables.pdf. FY2013 Operating Plan is from NIH Office of Budget, "Operating Plan—Allocation by IC," http://officeofbudget.od.nih.gov/cy.html. FY2014 Senate Committee is from S. 1284 and S.Rept. 113-71.

Notes: Totals may differ from the sum of the components due to rounding.

a. NIH FY2012 appropriations were provided in Division F (Labor/HHS/ Education) and Division E (Interior/Environment) of the Consolidated Appropriations Act, 2012 (P.L. 112-74). Amounts shown reflect across-the-board rescissions of 0.189% (Division F) and 0.16% (Division E). FY2012 reflects Secretary's transfer of $8.727 million to Health Resources and Services Administration for Ryan White AIDS and Secretary's net transfer of $18.273 million for Alzheimer's disease research to National Institute on Aging (NIA) from other ICs. FY2012 figures are shown on a comparable basis to FY2014, reflecting transfers from ICs to National Library of Medicine (NLM).

b. FY2013 Operating Plan reflects final funding levels under P.L. 113-6, the Consolidated and Further Continuing Appropriations Act, 2013 (which provided a program level total of $30.877 billion), reduced by the March 1, 2013, sequestration (-$1.553 billion) and the April 3, 2013, administrative transfers (-$173 million). FY2013 IC and NLM amounts are not comparable to FY2012 and FY2014 as the FY2013 figures do not reflect transfers from ICs to NLM.

c. Amounts for the National Institute of Diabetes and Digestive and Kidney Diseases (NIDDK) do not include mandatory funding for type 1 diabetes research (see note f).

d. The FY2014 request shifts a $27 million program on HIV/AIDS behavioral health research from the National Institute of Mental Health (NIMH) to the National Institute of Allergy and Infectious Diseases (NIAID). The Senate committee concurred, noting that the resulting decrease in NIMH funding did not reflect a cut to core NIMH activities.

e. This is a separate account in the Interior/Environment appropriations for National Institute of Environmental Health Sciences (NIEHS) research activities related to Superfund. FY2014 Senate Committee amount reflects a draft subcommittee bill released Aug. 1, 2013.

f. Mandatory funds available to NIDDK for type 1 diabetes research under PHS Act §330B (provided by P.L. 111-309 and P.L. 112-240). Funds have been appropriated through FY2014.

g. Additional funds for NLM from PHS Evaluation Set-Aside (§241 of PHS Act).

Department of Energy[53]

The Administration has requested $12.618 billion in FY2014 for Department of Energy (DOE) R&D and related activities, including programs in three major categories: science, national security, and energy. This request is 13.1% more than the FY2012 appropriation of $11.159 billion. The House bill would provide $9.888 billion. The Senate committee recommended $12.219 billion. (See **Table 9** for details.)

The request for the DOE Office of Science is $5.153 billion, an increase of 4.4% from the FY2012 appropriation of $4.935 billion. There is no authorized funding level for the Office of Science in FY2014; the most recent authorization act (the America COMPETES Reauthorization Act of 2010, P.L. 111-358) authorized appropriations through FY2013. The House bill would provide $4.653 billion. According to the Administration, the House funding level for the Office of Science "would eliminate all funding for new grants and likely lead to terminations of ongoing awards ... operations at all major scientific user facilities would be reduced or would cease."[54] The Senate committee recommended the requested amount.

The Obama Administration's previous goal of doubling the combined funding of the Office of Science and two other agencies is now "a commitment to increase funding" for those agencies.[55] For further discussion of the doubling goal and how it has evolved through successive Administrations and congressional action, see the section "Efforts to Double Certain R&D Accounts" above. The original target announced by the Bush Administration was to achieve the doubling in the decade from FY2006 to FY2016. The FY2014 request for the Office of Science is 42% more than its FY2006 baseline. The House and Senate committee recommendations are respectively 28% and 42% above the baseline.

The Office of Science includes six major research programs. The request of $1.862 billion for the largest program, basic energy sciences (BES), is an increase of $218 million relative to $1.645 billion in FY2012. The House bill would provide $1.583 billion. The Senate committee recommended $1.805 billion. Within BES, DOE plans to issue a solicitation in FY2014 for new Energy Frontier Research Centers (EFRCs) and renewals of existing centers. The request includes an increase of $69 million for EFRCs, to a total of $169 million, to allow DOE to forward-fund some of the new and renewed centers. The House bill would provide $60 million for EFRCs. The Senate committee recommended $100 million. Also in BES, the request includes an increase of $151 million for scientific user facilities; this would mostly fund increased operations at existing DOE synchrotron light sources. Requested construction funding for the BES-funded National Synchrotron Light Source II would decrease $125 million in FY2014 as the project nears completion. Meanwhile, requested funding for the Linac Coherent Light Source II (LCLS-II) would increase $65 million as project construction begins. The House bill would provide $47.5

---

[53] This section was written by Daniel Morgan, Specialist in Science and Technology Policy, CRS Resources, Science, and Industry Division.

[54] Executive Office of the President, Office of Management and Budget, Statement of Administration Policy on H.R. 2609, July 8, 2013.

[55] Executive Office of the President, "The President's Plan for Science and Innovation: Increasing Funding for Key Science Agencies in the 2014 Budget," http://www.whitehouse.gov/sites/default/files/microsites/ostp/2014_R&Dbudget_agencies.pdf. Compare Executive Office of the President, "The President's Plan for Science and Innovation: Doubling Funding for Key Science Agencies in the 2013 Budget," http://www.whitehouse.gov/sites/default/files/microsites/ostp/fy2013rd_doubling.pdf, and similar documents in previous years.

million less than the request for LCLS-II. In the BES Materials Sciences and Engineering program, the request includes $8.5 million for the Experimental Program to Stimulate Competitive Research (EPSCoR). The House bill would provide no funding for EPSCoR. The Senate committee recommended $20 million.

In the Office of Science fusion energy sciences program, the request would increase the U.S. contribution to the International Thermonuclear Experimental Reactor (ITER) from $105 million in FY2012 to $225 million in FY2014. In 2008, the cost for the U.S. share of ITER, a multi-year international construction project, was estimated to be between $1.45 billion and $2.2 billion. Schedule delays, design and scope changes, and other factors have likely increased ITER costs and delayed formal approval of a revised cost estimate. Pending a new official estimate, DOE believes that funding of $225 million per year will allow it to meet its international obligations, up to the achievement of ITER's intermediate "first plasma" milestone, for a total cost of $2.4 billion. The requested increase for U.S. ITER funding in FY2014 would be partly offset by a decrease in funding for domestic fusion activities. In particular, no FY2014 funding is requested for research or operations at the Alcator C-Mod tokamak, a fusion reactor that is scheduled to be shut down in FY2013. The House bill would provide $7.5 million less than the request for the U.S. contribution to ITER, but $55 million more than the request for domestic fusion activities, including $22 million for FY2014 operations and research at Alcator C-Mod. The Senate committee recommended $183.5 million for the U.S. contribution to ITER, contingent on submission of a baseline cost, schedule, and scope estimate. The Senate committee's recommended total for fusion energy sciences was the requested amount and included no funding for Alcator C-Mod.

The request for biological and environmental research in the Office of Science is $625 million, up 5.6% from $592 million in FY2012. This total is divided approximately evenly between two programs: biological systems science and climate and environmental sciences. The House bill would provide $494 million for biological and environmental research. The House committee report stated that "the Committee continues to support the Biological Systems Science program"; it did not mention the climate and environmental sciences program. The Senate committee recommended the requested amount for both programs.

The request for DOE national security R&D is $3.283 billion, a 5.8% increase from $3.103 billion in FY2012. The House bill would provide $3.209 billion, while the Senate committee recommended $3.398 billion. Most of the requested increase is in the Naval Reactors program. An increase of $97 million for Naval Reactors operations and infrastructure would fund recapitalization of facilities, infrastructure, and capital equipment. Naval Reactors construction funding would increase by $30 million and is projected to increase further in future years as construction begins on the Spent Fuel Handling Recapitalization project. The House bill includes $93 million less than the request for Naval Reactors operations and infrastructure and does not include funding for the Spent Fuel Handling Recapitalization project. The Senate committee recommended $66 million more than the request for Naval Reactors, with increases spread across several activities. In the Defense Nuclear Nonproliferation account, a requested increase of $41 million for R&D results largely from the assumption of certain costs for nuclear detection satellites that were previously paid by the Department of Defense. The House bill would provide the requested amount for nuclear nonproliferation R&D; the Senate committee recommended an increase of $20 million for the development of advanced nuclear detection technologies. In the Weapons Activities account, the Administration request would increase funding for nuclear weapons science and reduce funding for research on inertial confinement fusion and advanced simulation and computing. The House bill and the Senate committee recommendation would both increase funding for inertial confinement fusion, rather than decreasing it. Other Weapons Activities reductions in the Senate bill are largely a result of accounting changes.

The request for DOE energy R&D is $4.182 billion, up 34.0% from $3.121 billion in FY2012. The House bill would provide $2.026 billion. The Senate committee recommendation was $3.668 billion. The request would increase funding for R&D in the Office of Energy Efficiency and Renewable Energy (EERE) by 53%, from $1.653 billion in FY2012 to $2.528 billion in FY2014, with increases requested for most EERE programs. The House bill would provide $786 million and rescind $157 million in unobligated balances from prior years.[56] The Senate committee recommended $2.034 billion. Within EERE, Advanced Manufacturing (formerly Industrial Technologies) would receive $365 million under the request, more than triple its FY2012 level. The Advanced Manufacturing request includes $177 million to create Clean Energy Manufacturing Innovation Institutes (consistent with the previously discussed "National Network for Manufacturing Innovation"). Other focus areas for requested funding increases in EERE include batteries and energy storage, concentrating solar power, a demonstration of commercial-scale biofuels production under the Defense Production Act,[57] and grid integration for energy efficient buildings. Under the House bill, nearly every EERE program would decrease relative to FY2012, with Advanced Manufacturing ($120 million, up about 6% from FY2012) being a rare exception. The Senate committee recommended $126 million for Advanced Manufacturing. Also in EERE, the Senate committee directed DOE to terminate the Energy Efficient Buildings Hub, which it said has shown "no measurable benefit." The Administration's proposed increase in funding for fossil energy R&D reflects the rescission of unobligated prior-year balances in FY2012. Excluding this rescission, the FY2014 request for fossil energy R&D is a decrease of $95 million, mostly from the coal program. Funding for fossil energy R&D in the House bill would be $39 million more than the request, but would include $43 million less than requested for carbon capture. The request for the Advanced Research Projects Agency–Energy (ARPA-E) is $379 million, an increase of $104 million or 38%. The House bill would provide $70 million for ARPA-E, including the House committee recommendation of $50 million and a $20 million increase provided by a floor amendment. Despite this reduction in funding, the House committee report stated that the committee "remains supportive of ARPA-E's efforts." The Senate committee recommended the requested amount for ARPA-E.

---

[56] The House committee recommendation was $811 million. Two House floor amendments reduced funding for the Renewable Energy, Energy Reliability, and Efficiency account by a total of $25 million without specifying the activities within the account to which the reductions should apply. The figure of $786 million given here assumes that the full $25 million reduction is applied to EERE R&D, which is the largest activity in the account.

[57] See CRS Report R42568, *The Navy Biofuel Initiative Under the Defense Production Act*, by Anthony Andrews et al.

Table 9. Department of Energy R&D and Related Activities

(budget authority in millions of dollars)

	FY2012 Actual	FY2013 Enacted	FY2014 Request	FY2014 House	FY2014 Senate Committee
Science	**$4,935**	**$4,866**	**$5,153**	**$4,653**	**$5,153**
Basic Energy Sciences	1,645	—	1,862	1,583	1,805
High Energy Physics	771	—	777	773	807
Biological and Environmental Research	592	—	625	494	625
Nuclear Physics	535	—	570	552	570
Advanced Scientific Computing Research	428	—	466	432	494
Fusion Energy Sciences	393	—	458	506	458
Other	571	—	395	313	394
National Security	**3,103**	**3,245**	**3,283**	**3,209**	**3,398**
Weapons Activities[a]	1,665	1,688	1,624	1,697	1,653
Naval Reactors	1,080	1,080	1,246	1,109	1,312
Defense Nuclear Nonproliferation R&D	348	466	389	389	409
Defense Environmental Cleanup Tech. Dev.	10	11	24	14	24
Energy	**3,121**	**3,315**	**4,182**	**2,026**	**3,668**
Energy Efficiency and Renewable Energy[b]	1,653	1,661[c]	2,528	786[d]	2,034
Electricity Delivery & Energy Reliability R&D	96	99	119	64	99
Fossil Energy R&D	337	533	421	450	421
Nuclear Energy	760	757	735	656	735
Advanced Research Projects Agency–Energy	275	264	379	70	379
Total	**11,159**	**11,426**	**12,618**	**9,888**	**12,219**

Source: FY2012 actual and FY2014 request from DOE's FY2014 congressional budget justification, http://energy.gov/cfo/downloads/fy-2014-budget-justification. FY2013 enacted from P.L. 113-6 and explanatory statement, *Congressional Record*, March 11, 2013, pp. S1308-S1310. FY2014 House from H.R. 2609 as passed by the House and H.Rept. 113-135. FY2014 Senate from S. 1245 as reported and S.Rept. 113-47.

Notes: FY2013 enacted amounts are adjusted for the rescission in P.L. 113-6, Section 3004 (0.032% for security programs, 0.2% for nonsecurity programs, as determined by the Office of Management and Budget) but not for subsequent sequestration or reprogramming. Totals may differ from the sum of the components due to rounding.

a. Including Stockpile Services R&D Support, Stockpile Services R&D Certification and Safety, Science, Engineering except Enhanced Surety and Enhanced Surveillance, Inertial Confinement Fusion, Advanced Simulation and Computing, and National Security Applications. Additional R&D activities may take place in the subprograms of Directed Stockpile Work that are devoted to specific weapon systems, but these funds are not included in the table because detailed funding schedules for those subprograms are classified.

b. Excluding Weatherization and Intergovernmental Activities.

c. Estimated by CRS because an amount for Weatherization and Intergovernmental Activities was not specified in P.L. 113-6 or its explanatory statement.

d. Not adjusted for rescission of $157 million in unobligated prior-year balances. House floor amendments reduced funding for Renewable Energy, Energy Reliability, and Efficiency by a total of $25 million without specifying the activities within that account to which the reductions should apply. In this table, the full $25 million reduction is assumed to apply to energy efficiency and renewable energy R&D, which is the account's largest activity.

National Science Foundation[58]

The National Science Foundation (NSF) supports basic research and education in the non-medical sciences and engineering. Congress established the Foundation as an independent federal agency in 1950 and directed it to "promote the progress of science; to advance the national health, prosperity, and welfare; to secure the national defense; and for other purposes."[59] The NSF is a primary source of federal support for U.S. university research, especially in certain fields such as mathematics and computer science. It is also responsible for significant shares of the federal science, technology, engineering, and mathematics (STEM) education program portfolio and federal STEM student aid and support.

For FY2014 the Administration seeks $7.626 billion in funding for the NSF. This amount is $521.1 million (7.3%) more than the FY2012 actual level of $7.105 billion. The House Committee on Appropriations recommends a total of $6.995 billion for NSF in FY2014. The Senate Committee on Appropriations recommends a total of $7.426 billion. Congress has not enacted specific FY2014 appropriations authorizations for NSF.[60] For additional detail on NSF funding levels, including FY2013 current plan estimates, see **Table 10**.

In its budget documents NSF indicates that its overarching priorities for FY2014 include the following six programs.

- *Cyber-enabled Materials, Manufacturing, and Smart Systems (CEMMSS)*—The FY2014 request is $300.4 million, which is $156.1 million (108.2%) more than the FY2012 actual amount of $144.3 million.

- *Cyberinfrastructure Framework for 21st Century Science, Engineering, and Education (CIF21)*—The FY2014 request is $155.5 million, which is $64.2 million (70.4%) more than the FY2012 actual amount of $91.2 million.

- *NSF Innovation Corps (I-Corps)*—The FY2014 request is $24.9 million, which is $18.1 million (267.1%) more than the FY2012 actual amount of $6.8 million.

- *Integrated NSF Support Promoting Interdisciplinary Research and Education (INSPIRE)*—The FY2014 request is $63.0 million, which is $33.9 million (116.5%) more than the FY2012 actual amount of $29.1 million.

- *Science, Engineering, and Education for Sustainability (SEES)*—The FY2014 request is $222.8 million, which is $65.3 million (41.4%) more than the FY2012 actual amount of $157.6 million.

- *Secure and Trustworthy Cyberspace (SaTC)*—The FY2014 request is $110.3 million, which is $3.1 million (2.8%) less than the FY2012 actual amount of $113.4 million.

---

[58] This section was written by Heather B. Gonzalez, Specialist in Science and Technology Policy, CRS Resources, Science, and Industry Division. Numbers are rounded. Data available upon request.

[59] The National Science Foundation Act of 1950 (P.L. 81-507).

[60] NSF relies on its organic act for budget authority in FY2014.

Since FY2006, overall increases in the NSF budget have been at least partially driven by the so-called "doubling path policy." Congress and successive Administrations have sought to double funding for the NSF, Department of Energy's Office of Science, and National Institute of Standards and Technology's core laboratory and construction accounts (collectively "the targeted accounts"). However, actual funding for the targeted accounts has not typically reached authorized levels during the authorization period, which ends in FY2013.[61] It is unclear if policymakers will seek to continue the doubling path policy in FY2014. In FY2013 some legislators expressed concern about pursuing the doubling effort given the nation's fiscal challenges, including one who urged observers "to be realistic about the notion of doubling the NSF budget."[62] Other analysts have asserted that without the doubling path policy in place, funding levels for targeted accounts might have fallen over the past half-decade.[63]

Congress typically appropriates to NSF at the major account level. NSF's major accounts are Research and Related Activities (R&RA); Education and Human Resources (E&HR); Major Research Equipment and Facilities Construction (MREFC); Agency Operations and Awards Management (AOAM); National Science Board (NSB); and the Office of Inspector General (IG).[64]

R&RA is the largest NSF account and the primary source of research funding at the NSF.[65] The Administration seeks $6.212 billion in funding for R&RA in FY2014; noting "strong support for cross-cutting research priorities such as advanced manufacturing, clean energy and sustainability, break-through materials, robotics, cyberinfrastructure, and cybersecurity." The FY2014 request for R&RA is $454.0 million (7.9%) more than the FY2012 actual funding level of $5.758 billion. The House Committee on Appropriations recommends $5.676 billion for R&RA in FY2014. The Senate Committee on Appropriations recommends $6.018 billion. NSF consolidated certain R&RA sub-accounts in FY2013, moving from 11 directorates and offices to 8.[66]

Compared to FY2012 enacted levels, the FY2014 request for R&RA includes increases for all but one major sub-account.[67] As was the case in FY2013, the largest increase—by both amount ($138.0 million) and percentage (34.6% more than the FY2012 level of $398.6 million)—is in the International and Integrative Activities account (IIA), for which the Administration seeks $536.6 million in FY2014. Also as with FY2013, over half of the growth in IIA is attributable to requested increases in funding for the Graduate Research Fellowship (GRF).[68] The second-largest

---

[61] The most recent authorization levels for the targeted accounts, specified in the America COMPETES Reauthorization Act (P.L. 111-358), were for FY2011, FY2012, and FY2013.

[62] Opening Statement of Ranking Member Dan Lipinksi, in U.S. Congress, House Committee on Science, Space, and Technology, Subcommittee on Research and Science Education, "The National Science Foundation's FY2013 Budget Request," hearings, 112th Cong., 2nd sess., February 28, 2012.

[63] Testimony of Dr. Jeffrey L. Furman, in U.S. Congress, Senate Committee on Commerce, Science, and Transportation, "Five Years of the America COMPETES Act: Progress, Challenges, and Next Steps," hearings, 112th Cong., 2nd sess., September 19, 2012.

[64] Funds from major NSF accounts may be merged at the program level and in many cases NSF's education, facilities, and research activities are deeply integrated as a matter of practice.

[65] For more information on historical funding trends at NSF, see CRS Report R42470, *An Analysis of STEM Education Funding at the NSF: Trends and Policy Discussion*, by Heather B. Gonzalez.

[66] The FY2014 NSF budget request adjusts funding levels for all reported years to account for this change.

[67] The FY2014 NSF budget request decreases funding for the U.S. Artic Research Commission by about -3.4%, from $1.45 million in FY2012 to $1.40 million in FY2014.

[68] The FY2014 NSF budget request seeks $162.6 million for the R&RA contribution to the GRF. This amount is $74.1 (continued...)

---

increase—by amount ($86.6 million) and percentage (10.5% over the FY2012 level of $824.6 million)—goes to the Engineering (ENG) directorate. The Administration seeks $911.1 million for ENG in FY2014. About a third of the growth in the ENG account stems from requested increases for small business research programs in ENG's Division of Industrial Innovation and Partnerships (IIP).[69]

The House report[70] provides $13.9 million for new investments in cognitive science and neuroscience research, offers the requested levels for various (unspecified) R&RA advanced manufacturing proposals, and supports a temporary reduction in Antarctic research funding in order to provide funds for the implementation of certain recommended safety and management changes. The Senate report[71] directs NSF to apply the $194.0 million reduction to R&RA (from the requested level) to the so-called OneNSF initiatives.[72] Among other things, the Senate report also provides the full request for SEES ($222.8 million).

Other widely tracked sub-accounts in the R&RA account include Experimental Program to Stimulate Competitive Research (EPSCoR), the Division of Astronomical Sciences (AST), and the Directorate on Social, Behavioral, and Economic Sciences (SBE). The FY2014 request for EPSCoR is $163.6 million; or $12.7 million (8.4%) more than the FY2012 actual level of $150.9 million. The FY2014 request for AST is $243.6 million, or $8.9 million (3.8%) more than the FY2012 actual level of $234.7 million. The FY2014 request for SBE is $272.4 million. This amount is $18.2 million, or 7.1%, more than the FY2012 actual funding level of $254.2 million.

The Senate report provides $163.6 million to EPSCoR in FY2014. The House report is silent on the question of FY2014 funding for EPSCoR. With respect to AST, the Senate report states that the committee "expects NSF to fully support the scientific and education activities at the Division of Astronomical Sciences," including funding for the National Radio Astronomy Observatory at FY2012 levels and full support of instruments and facilities. The House report does not specify funding for AST.

The Administration seeks $880.3 million in funding for E&HR in FY2014. This amount is $49.8 million (6.0%) more than the FY2012 actual level of $830.5 million. E&HR is the primary source of funding for science, technology, engineering, and mathematics (STEM) education at the NSF. Approximately 44.0% of the FY2014 request for E&HR (or $387.0 million) would support research and development activities. In FY2012, FY2011, and FY2010 (all actual) the percentage of E&HR funding that supported R&D was 30.3%, 25.9%, and 13.7%, respectively. The House

---

(...continued)

million (83.7%) more than the FY2012 actual R&RA funding level of $88.5 million. E&HR also contributes to the GRF.

[69] The FY2014 request for IIP is $225.5. This amount is $37.7 million (20.1%) more that the FY2012 actual level of $187.8 million. About 80% of this increase would support growth in the NSF Small Business Innovation Research (SBIR) and Small Business Technology Transfer (STTR) programs. For more information on these programs, see CRS Report 96-402, *Small Business Innovation Research (SBIR) Program*, by Wendy H. Schacht.

[70] This section refers to H.Rept. 113-171, which accompanied H.R. 2787 (Commerce, Justice, Science, and Related Agencies Appropriations Bill, 2014) when it was reported from committee, as the "House report."

[71] This section refers to S.Rept. 113-78, which accompanied S. 1329 (Commerce and Justice, and Science, and Related Agencies Appropriations Bill, 2014) when it was reported from committee, as the "Senate report."

[72] It is not clear how this directive might be applied in practice. The FY2014 budget request does not include the term "OneNSF." However, NSF described the six programs identified as "FY2014 Priorities" in its FY2014 budget request (e.g., CEMMSS, CIF21, SEES, etc.) as "OneNSF" initiatives in its FY2013 budget request.

report recommends $825.0 million for E&HR in FY2014. The Senate report recommends the requested level.

As mentioned earlier in "Reorganization of STEM Education Programs," for FY2014 the Administration proposes a reorganization and consolidation of many federal STEM education programs.[73] Under the Administration's plan, NSF would play a leadership role in the federal undergraduate and graduate STEM education efforts. The Department of Education and Smithsonian Institution would focus on K-12 education and informal STEM education, respectively. The foundation's FY2014 budget request highlights several NSF changes associated with the Administration's plan for reorganization of the federal STEM education effort. These include establishment of the Catalyzing Advances in Undergraduate STEM Education (CAUSE) program;[74] expansion of the GRF such that it would become a primary source for all federal research fellowships; and the creation of the NSF Research Traineeship (NRT), which would replace the Integrative Graduate Education Research Traineeship (IGERT). It is unclear how the expansion of the GRF—which would become the National Graduate Research Fellowship (NGRF)—would affect the availability of fellowships for mission-driven research at other federal science agencies. The Administration seeks $123.1 million in funding for CAUSE, $325.1 million for the NGRF, and $55.1 million for the NRT in FY2014.

Both the House and Senate reports reject the proposed reorganization plan for programs within the purview of the FY2014 Commerce, Justice, Science, and Related Agencies appropriations act. The House report notes that there may be individual instances in which the Committee accepts a change. The Senate report defers action on the reorganization until the Office of Science and Technology Policy (OSTP) finalizes STEM education program assessments as required by the America COMPETES Reauthorization Act of 2010 (P.L. 111-358).The House report also specifically rejects the establishment of the CAUSE program or the change to a federal government-wide GRF program. The Senate report asks NSF to work with OSTP on "how NSF could implement a broader program for graduate and undergraduate programs across the entire Federal Government, and to identify which programs across Government could benefit from such a program."[75]

Other accounts that fund R&D at the NSF include the Major Research Equipment and Facilities Construction (MREFC) account. The FY2014 request for the MREFC account is $210.1 million. This amount is $12.0 million (6.1%) more than the FY2012 actual funding level of $198.1 million.[76] NSF indicates that FY2014 funding would provide a final year of support for the Advanced Interferometer Gravitational-Wave Observatory (AdvLIGO) and Ocean Observatories Initiative (OOI), as well as the first year of funding for the Large Synoptic Survey Telescope (LSST). Funding for the Advanced Technology Solar Telescope and National Ecological Observatory Network (NEON) would continue. The House report provides an amount ($182.6 million) that is equal to the funding request for continuing projects, but that would not cover costs

---

[73] Although the details of the plan appear to be in flux, the Administration proposes reducing the number of federal STEM education programs by about 50% and shifting approximately $180.0 million in budget authority from various federal agencies to the NSF, Department of Education, and Smithsonian Institution. Some programs within the three receiving agencies would also be consolidated, as would STEM education programs at other federal agencies.

[74] The CAUSE program would consolidate three E&HR programs, three R&RA programs, and one NSF-wide program.

[75] S.Rept. 113-78, p. 124.

[76] As authorized by P.L. 112-55, NSF transferred $30.0 million from the R&RA account to MREFC in FY2012. This amount is reflected in the FY2013 request, which is $30.0 million more than the level Congress specified in FY2012.

---

of the first year of construction for the LSST. The Senate report provides the requested level and welcomes the start of LSST construction.

The Administration seeks $304.3 million, $4.5 million, and $14.3 million, respectively, for AOAM, NSB, and OIG in FY2014. These amounts are between 1.6% and 1.7% more than the FY2012 actual funding levels for these accounts. The House report provides $294.0 million for AOAM; the Senate report provides about $4.0 million more.

The FY2014 NSF budget request also includes funding for three multi-agency initiatives: National Nanotechnology Initiative (NNI, $430.9 million), Networking and Information Technology Research and Development (NITRD, $1.227 billion), and U.S. Global Change Research Program (USGCRP, $326.4 million). The request for NNI is $35.4 million (7.6%) less than the FY2012 actual amount of $466.3 million; the NITRD request is $11.2 million (0.9%) more than the FY2012 funding level of $1.216 billion; and the request for USGCRP is $7.0 million (12.1%) below the FY2012 actual level of $333.4 million.

Table 10. NSF Funding by Major Account

(budget authority in millions of dollars)

Account	FY2012 Actual	FY2013 Current Plan[a]	FY2014 Request	FY2014 House Committee	FY2014 Senate Committee
Biological Sciences	$712.3	$678.9	$760.6	*n/a*	*n/a*
Computer and Information Science and Engineering[b]	937.2	858.5	950.3	*n/a*	*n/a*
Engineering	824.6	813.5	911.1	*n/a*	*n/a*
Geosciences[b]	1,321.4	1,265.8	1393.9	*n/a*	*n/a*
Mathematical and Physical Sciences	1,308.7	1,249.5	1386.1	*n/a*	*n/a*
Social, Behavioral, and Economic Sciences	254.2	242.5	272.4	*n/a*	*n/a*
International and Integrative Activities[b]	398.6	433.5	536.6	*n/a*	*n/a*
U.S. Arctic Research Commission	1.45	1.4	1.4	*n/a*	*n/a*

Account	FY2012 Actual	FY2013 Current Plan[a]	FY2014 Request	FY2014 House Committee	FY2014 Senate Committee
Research and Related Activities, Total	**$5,758.3**	**$5,543.7**	**$6,212.3**	**$5,676.2**	**$6,018.3**
Education and Human Resources	830.5	833.3	880.3	825.0	880.3
Major Research Equipment and Facilities Construction	198.1	196.2	210.1	182.6	210.1
Agency Operations and Award Management	299.3	293.6	304.3	294.0	298.4
National Science Board	4.4	4.1	4.5	4.1	4.5
Office of the Inspector General	14.1	13.2	14.3	13.2	14.3
NSF, Total	**$7,105.4[c]**	**$6,884.1**	**$7,625.8**	**$6,995.1**	**$7,425.9**

Source: Numbers in the "FY2012 Actual" and "FY2014 Request" columns are from the FY2014 *NSF Budget Request to Congress*. Numbers in the "FY2013 Current Plan" column are from the National Science Foundation website. Numbers in the columns titled, "FY2014 House Cte." and "FY2014 Senate Cte." are from House and Senate committee reports on Commerce, Justice, Science, and Related Agencies funding for FY2014, respectively.

Notes: The term "n/a" means not available. Numbers are rounded. Totals may differ from the sum of the components due to rounding.

a. FY2013 NSF current plan estimates include reductions required by the sequester and by applicable rescissions in P.L. 113-6 (Consolidated and Further Continuing Appropriations Act, 2013).

b. On September 7, 2012, NSF announced that it was realigning the Research and Related Activities account. Under the new account structure, the Office of Cyberinfrastructure became a division within the Directorate for Computer and Information Science and Engineering and the Office of Polar Programs became a division within the Geosciences directorate. The offices of International Science and Engineering and Integrative Activities have merged to become the Office of International and Integrative Activities.

c. Total includes $0.7 million in OIG FY2012 ARRA (American Recovery and Reinvestment Act, P.L. 111-5) actual obligations.

National Aeronautics and Space Administration[77]

The Administration has requested $16.516 billion for NASA R&D in FY2014. This amount is 6.6% more than the $15.491 billion in NASA's operating plan for FY2013.[78] The House committee recommended $15.297 billion. The Senate committee recommended $16.794 billion. For a breakdown of these amounts, see **Table 11**. There is no authorized level for NASA funding in FY2014; the most recent authorization act (the NASA Authorization Act of 2010, P.L. 111-267) authorized appropriations through FY2013. Bills that would authorize FY2014 appropriations for NASA include H.R. 2687, H.R. 2616, and S. 1317.

The FY2014 request for Science is $5.018 billion, a 4.9% increase from the FY2013 operating plan. The House and Senate committees recommended $4.781 billion and $5.154 billion respectively. In Planetary Science, the request includes $40.5 million for observation of near-Earth objects and $50 million for management of a Department of Energy (DOE) program to produce plutonium-238, which some spacecraft use for power generation. In the past, congressional policymakers have disagreed about whether NASA or DOE should fund DOE production of plutonium-238 for NASA. The House and Senate committee recommendations for Planetary Science were respectively $1.315 billion and $1.318 billion. Among other differences relative to the request, the House committee recommended increases for exploration of Mars and the outer planets and no funding for plutonium-238 production. The Senate committee's recommended increase was entirely for Mars exploration. In Earth Science, the request includes $30 million to begin development of future land imaging capabilities to replace the current Landsat satellites, operated by the U.S. Geological Survey, as well as funds to assume responsibility for certain Earth-observing satellite instruments previously held by the National Oceanographic and Atmospheric Administration (NOAA). The House committee recommended $1.659 billion for Earth Science, and its report stated that no funds should be spent on the proposed Landsat and NOAA-related activities. The Senate committee recommended approximately the requested amount for Earth Science, including the requested funds for land imaging, but its report expressed concern about the Administration's approach and directed NASA to submit a plan for implementing future Landsat satellites at substantially lower cost. The request for the James Webb Space Telescope (JWST) is $658.2 million. NASA expects FY2014 to be the peak funding year for JWST and states that the budget and schedule for the JWST program remain consistent with the 2011 revised plan. In the FY2012 appropriations conference report, Congress capped the formulation and development cost of JWST and mandated annual reports on the program by the Government Accountability Office. The House committee recommended $584.0 million for JWST in FY2014, while the Senate committee recommended the requested amount.

The request for Aeronautics is $565.7 million, a 6.8% increase from the FY2013 operating plan. The request for Integrated Systems Research includes a new program on advanced composite materials and structures. In the Fundamental Aeronautics program, NASA plans to explore options for the future of its rotorcraft research; this planning will be coordinated with other

---

[77] This section was written by Daniel Morgan, Specialist in Science and Technology Policy, CRS Resources, Science, and Industry Division.

[78] Based on the August 29, 2013, NASA operating plan, which reflects numerous changes to the enacted FY2013 amounts as the result of rescissions, sequestration, transfers, and reprogramming.

government agencies and industry partners. The House committee recommended $566.0 million for Aeronautics, while the Senate committee recommended $558.7 million.

For Space Technology, the Administration has requested $742.6 million, a 20.8% increase from the FY2013 operating plan. The requested increase is largely explained by existing projects that are moving from the planning and design phase to the more expensive tasks of hardware manufacture and demonstration. The request also includes funds to accelerate the development of high-power solar electric propulsion technology for future spacecraft. The House and Senate committee recommendations were respectively $576.0 million and $670.1 million.

The Administration's request for Exploration in FY2014 is $3.916 billion, an increase of 5.7% from the FY2013 operating plan. This account funds development of the Orion Multipurpose Crew Vehicle (MPCV) and the Space Launch System (SLS) heavy-lift rocket, which were mandated by the 2010 authorization act for human exploration beyond Earth orbit. The account also funds development of a commercial crew transportation capability for future U.S. astronaut access to the International Space Station. Relative to the FY2013 operating plan, the request of $821.4 million for commercial crew is an increase of 56.5%, while the request of $2.730 billion for Orion, the SLS, and related ground systems (known collectively as Exploration Systems Development) is a decrease of 5.3%. In the past, this apparent difference in human spaceflight priorities between Congress and the Administration has been controversial. According to NASA, the amounts requested are consistent with the planned schedules for both Orion/SLS and commercial crew. NASA officials state that the request for commercial crew is necessary to make commercial crew transportation services available in 2017, while the request for Orion and SLS is sufficient for an uncrewed flight of the SLS in 2017 and a crewed flight in 2021. The House committee recommended $3.612 billion, including $500 million for commercial crew and $2.825 billion for Exploration Systems Development. The Senate committee recommended $4.209 billion, including $775 for commercial crew and $3.118 billion for Exploration Systems Development.

The request for the International Space Station (ISS) is $3.049 billion, an increase of 9.8% from the FY2013 operating plan. The ISS account includes the cost of commercial cargo flights for ISS resupply. The first such flight was in May 2012. A second provider is expected to attempt its first cargo resupply flight in 2013. The House committee recommended $2.860 billion. The Senate committee recommended the requested amount.

NASA has proposed a mission to capture a small asteroid robotically, redirect it into orbit around the Moon, and explore it with astronauts as one of the first destinations for Orion and the SLS. The FY2014 budget request includes initial funding for this mission in three different accounts: $20 million in Science for identification and characterization of a suitable asteroid, $45 million in Exploration for mission definition and planning and development of capture mechanisms, and $40 million in Space Technology for development of the solar electric propulsion technology that would be used to redirect the asteroid's orbit. The House report called the proposed asteroid mission "premature" and stated that the House committee's recommendation "does not include any of the requested increases associated with the asteroid retrieval proposal."

Table 11. NASA R&D

(budget authority in millions of dollars)

	FY2012 Actual	FY2013 Op. Plan	FY2014 Request	FY2014 House Cte.	FY2014 Senate Cte.
Science	$5,073.7	$4,781.6	$5,017.8	$4,781.0	$5,154.2
Earth Science	*1,760.5*	*1,659.2*	*1,846.1*	*1,659.0*	*1,846.2*
Planetary Science	*1,501.4*	*1,271.5*	*1,217.5*	*1,315.0*	*1,317.6*
Astrophysics	*648.4*	*617.0*	*642.3*	*622.0*	*678.4*
James Webb Space Telescope	*518.6*	*627.6*	*658.2*	*584.0*	*658.2*
Heliophysics	*644.8*	*606.3*	*653.7*	*601.0*	*653.8*
Aeronautics	569.4	529.5	565.7	566.0	558.7
Space Technology	573.7	614.5	742.6	576.0	670.1
Exploration	3,707.3	3,705.5	3,915.5	3,612.0	4,209.3
Exploration Systems Development	*3,001.6*	*2,883.8*	*2,730.0*	*2,825.0*	*3,118.2*
Commercial Spaceflight	*406.0*	*525.0*	*821.4*	*500.0*	*775.0*
Exploration R&D	*299.7*	*296.7*	*364.2*	*287.0*	*316.1*
International Space Station	2,789.9	2,775.9	3,049.1	2,860.0	3,049.1
Subtotal R&D	**12,714.0**	**12,407.0**	**13,290.7**	**12,395.0**	**13,641.4**
Non-R&D Programs[a]	1,568.5	1,100.6	965.0	967.3	988.4
Cross-Agency Support	2,993.9	2,711.0	2,850.3	2,711.0	2,793.6
Associated with R&D[b]	*2,665.1*	*2,490.1*	*2,657.4*	*2,514.8*	*2,604.9*
Construction & Environmental C&R	494.5	646.6	609.4	525.0	586.9
Associated with R&D[b]	*440.2*	*593.9*	*568.1*	*487.0*	*547.2*
Total R&D	**15,819.3**	**15,491.0**	**16,516.2**	**15,396.7**	**16,793.5**
Total NASA	**17,770.0**	**16,865.2**	**17,715.4**	**16,598.3**	**18,010.3**

Sources: FY2012 actual and FY2014 request from NASA's FY2014 congressional budget justification, http://www.nasa.gov/news/budget/. FY2013 operating plan as of August 29, 2013, from http://www.nasa.gov/sites/default/files/files/FY13_op_plan_info_082913Aug.pdf. FY2013 House Committee from H.R. 2787 as reported and H.Rept. 113-171. FY2014 Senate Committee from S. 1329 as reported and S.Rept. 113-78.

Notes: Totals may differ from the sum of the components due to rounding.

a. Space Shuttle, Space and Flight Support, Education, and Inspector General.

b. Allocation between R&D and non-R&D is estimated by CRS in proportion to the underlying program amounts in order to allow calculation of a total for R&D. The Cross-Agency Support and Construction and Environmental Compliance and Remediation accounts consist mostly of indirect costs for other programs, assessed in proportion to their direct costs.

Department of Commerce

National Institute of Standards and Technology[79]

The National Institute of Standards and Technology (NIST) is a laboratory of the Department of Commerce with a mandate to increase the competitiveness of U.S. companies through appropriate support for industrial development of precompetitive, generic technologies and the diffusion of government-developed technological advances to users in all segments of the American economy. NIST research also provides the measurement, calibration, and quality assurance techniques that underpin U.S. commerce, technological progress, improved product reliability, manufacturing processes, and public safety.

The President's FY2014 budget requests $928.2 million for NIST, an increase of 23.6% ($177.4 million) over the FY2012 appropriation. Included in this figure is $693.7 million for research and development in the Scientific and Technical Research and Services (STRS) account, 22.3% ($126.7 million) above FY2012 funding. Under the Industrial Technology Services (ITS) account, the Manufacturing Extension Partnership (MEP) program is to receive $153.1 million, a 19.2% ($24.7 million) increase over FY2012. Also included in ITS is $21.4 million for the Advanced Manufacturing Technology Consortia (AMTech), which was not funded when it was included in the FY2012 budget. The $60.0 million for construction is 8.3% ($4.6 million) more than that provided in FY2012.

The House Committee on Appropriations report to accompany H.R. 2787 recommends funding NIST at $784.0 million, 15.5% below the budget request. The $609.0 million provided for the STRS account is 12.2% less than the Administration's proposal, while the $120.0 million for MEP is 21.6% below the President's figure. There is no funding provided for AMTech. The $55.0 million for construction is 8.3% less than the budget request.

The Senate Committee on Appropriations report to accompany S. 1329 includes $947.5 million for NIST, 2.1% more than proposed by the President. Funding for the STRS account would amount to $703.0 million, 1.3% higher than the budget request. Support for MEP would total $153.1 million, the same as the Administration's proposal; however, the $31.4 million for AMTech represents a 46.7% increase over the President's recommendation. The $60.0 million for construction is identical to the budget request.

In addition to the appropriations included in the budget proposal that are to be addressed through the annual appropriations process, the Administration includes two new programs that are to be funded through mandatory appropriations (spending that is typically "provided in permanent or multi-year appropriations contained in the authorizing law, and therefore, the funding becomes available automatically each year, without legislative action by Congress").[80] According to the budget request, NIST would receive $100 million generated by the proceeds of the spectrum auction to "conduct public safety R&D" as part of the Wireless Innovation (WIN) Fund (under provisions of the Middle Class Tax Relief and Job Creation Act of 2012). The President also

---

[79] This section was written by Wendy H. Schacht, Specialist in Science and Technology Policy, CRS Resources, Science, and Industry Division.

[80] See CRS Report RL33074, *Mandatory Spending Since 1962*, by Mindy R. Levit and D. Andrew Austin.

proposes $1.000 billion in support for the establishment of a National Network for Manufacturing Innovation.[81]

NIST's extramural programs (currently the Manufacturing Extension Partnership and AMTech), which are directed toward increased private sector commercialization, have been a source of contention. Some Members of Congress have expressed skepticism over a "technology policy" based on providing federal funds to industry for the development of "pre-competitive generic" technologies. This approach, coupled with pressures to balance the federal budget, has led to proposals for the elimination of these activities. In 2007, the Advanced Technology Program was terminated and replaced by the Technology Innovation Program which operated until support was withdrawn in the final FY2012 appropriation.[82]

Increases in spending for NIST laboratories that perform the research essential to the mission responsibilities of the agency have tended to remain small. As part of the American Competitiveness Initiative, announced by former President Bush in the 2006 State of the Union address, the Administration stated its intention to double funding over 10 years for "innovation-enabling research" done, in part, at NIST through its "core" programs (defined as the STRS account and the construction budget). In April 2009, President Obama indicated his decision to double the budget of key science agencies, including NIST, over the next 10 years. In President Obama's FY2011 budget the timeframe for doubling slipped to 11 years; his FY2012 budget was intentionally silent on a timeframe for doubling. There is no mention of doubling or a timeframe in the FY2014 budget request.

Table 12. NIST

(in millions of dollars)

NIST Program	FY2012 Enacted (P.L. 112-55)	FY2013 Enacted P.L. 113-6 (post-rescission, pre-sequestration)	FY2014 Request	FY2014 House Committee	FY2014 Senate Committee
Scientific and Technical Research and Services	567.0	599.5	693.7	609.0	703.0
Industrial Technology Services					
Technology Innovation Program	0	0	0	0	0
Manufacturing Extension Partnership	128.4	125.8	153.1	120.0	153.1
Baldrige Program	0	0	0	0	0
AMTech	0	14.2	21.4	0	31.4
Construction	55.4	58.8	60.0	55.0	60.0

---

[81] For additional information on the National Network for Manufacturing Innovation, see CRS Report R42625, *The Obama Administration's Proposal to Establish a National Network for Manufacturing Innovation*, by John F. Sargent Jr.

[82] For additional information on the MEP and TIP programs, see CRS Report RS22815, *The Technology Innovation Program*, by Wendy H. Schacht.

NIST Program	FY2012 Enacted (P.L. 112-55)	FY2013 Enacted P.L. 113-6 (post-rescission, pre-sequestration)	FY2014 Request	FY2014 House Committee	FY2014 Senate Committee
NIST Total	**750.8**	**807.1**	**928.2**	**784.0**	**947.5**
Mandatory Appropriations					
National Network for Manufacturing Innovation		0	1,000.0	0	0

Sources: NIST website (available at http://www.nist.gov/public_affairs/budget/index.cfm), P.L. 112-55, Administration's FY2014 Budget Request, House Rept. 113-171, and Senate Rept. 113-78.

Note: Totals may differ from the sum of the components due to rounding.

National Oceanic and Atmospheric Administration[83]

The Commerce Department's National Oceanic and Atmospheric Administration (NOAA) conducts scientific research in areas such as ecosystems, climate, global climate change, weather, and oceans; supplies information on the oceans and atmosphere; and manages coastal and marine organisms and environments. NOAA was created in 1970 by Reorganization Plan No. 4.[84] The reorganization was intended to unify elements of the nation's environmental activities and to provide a systematic approach for monitoring, analyzing, and protecting the environment.

NOAA's R&D efforts focus on three areas: climate; weather and air quality; and ocean, coastal, and Great Lakes resources. NOAA's R&D efforts support the four long-term goals of NOAA's Next Generation Strategic Plan: (1) climate adaptation and mitigation, (2) weather-ready nation,[85] (3) healthy oceans, and (4) resilient coastal communities and economies.[86]

For FY2014, President Obama has requested $733.0 million in R&D funding for NOAA, a 35.0% increase in funding from the FY2013 enacted level of $543.0 million. R&D accounts for 13.5% of NOAA's total FY2014 discretionary budget request of $5.440 billion. The R&D request consists of $503.9 million for research (68.7%), $65.7 million for development (9.0%), and $163.4 million for R&D equipment (22.3%). Excluding equipment, about $393 million (68.9%) of the R&D request would fund intramural programs and $177 million (31.1%) would fund extramural programs.[87]

---

[83] This section was written by Harold F. Upton, Analyst in Natural Resources Policy, CRS Resources, Science, and Industry Division.

[84] "Reorganization Plan No. 4 of 1970," 35 *Federal Register* 15627-15630, October 6, 1970; also, see http://www.lib.noaa.gov/noaainfo/heritage/ReorganizationPlan4 html.

[85] According to NOAA a weather-ready nation is envisioned as a society that is prepared for and responds to weather-related events.

[86] National Oceanic and Atmospheric Administration, *National Oceanic and Atmospheric Administration FY2014 Budget Summary*, National Oceanic and Atmospheric Administration, Washington, DC, April 2013, http://www.corporateservices noaa.gov/nbo/fy14_bluebook/FINALnoaaBlueBook_2014_Web_Full.pdf.

[87] National Oceanic and Atmospheric Administration, *National Oceanic and Atmospheric Administration FY2014 Budget Summary*, National Oceanic and Atmospheric Administration, Washington, DC, April 2013. http://www.corporateservices noaa.gov/nbo/fy14_bluebook/FINALnoaaBlueBook_2014_Web_Full.pdf.

NOAA's administrative structure has five line offices that reflect its diverse mission: National Ocean Service (NOS); National Marine Fisheries Service (NMFS); National Environmental Satellite, Data, and Information Service (NESDIS); National Weather Service (NWS); and Office of Oceanic and Atmospheric Research (OAR). In addition to NOAA's five line offices, Program Support (PS), a cross-cutting budget activity, includes the Office of Marine and Aviation Operations (OMAO).

OAR is the primary center for R&D within NOAA. In FY2013, OAR accounted for 61.9% of NOAA's R&D funding. The President's FY2014 request would provide OAR with $438.7 million in R&D funding which is 59.9% of total R&D funding requested by NOAA and 92.9% of OAR's total budget request of $472.4 million.

Table 13 provides R&D funding levels by line office for FY2012, FY2013, and the FY2014 request.[88] On July 18, 2013, the Senate Committee on Appropriations reported S. 1329, and on July 23, 2013, the House Committee on Appropriations reported H.R. 2787. Neither of the appropriations bills or accompanying committee reports specifies the R&D funding levels for NOAA, but total recommended agency and OAR funding has been provided in **Table 13** for context.

Table 13. NOAA R&D

(in millions of dollars)

Line Offices	FY2012 Enacted	FY2013 Enacted[a]	FY2014 Request	FY2014 House Committee	FY2014 Senate Committee
National Ocean Service	62.4	62.2	83.9	n/a	n/a
National Marine Fisheries Service	53.6	32.4	51.3	n/a	n/a
Office of Oceanic and Atmospheric Research	338.6	336.1	438.7	n/a	n/a
National Weather Service	22.5	24.3	40.2	n/a	n/a
National Environmental Satellite, Data, and Information Service	26.7	25.1	27.0	n/a	n/a
Office of Marine and Aviation Operations[b]	69.6	62.8	91.9	n/a	n/a
Total R&D	**573.4**	**543.0**	**733.0**	**n/a**	**n/a**
Total OAR	**382.9**	**369.4**	**472.4**	**358.5**	**456.5**
NOAA Total	**4,893.7**	**4,747.8**	**5,439.7**	**4,915.5**	**5,589.7**

Sources: Stacy Dennery, NOAA Budget Office, e-mail concerning NOAA R&D, August 7, 2013; NOAA Budget Office, e-mail concerning the FY2013 Spend Plan, July 22, 2013.

Notes: Totals may differ from the sum of the components due to rounding. n/a = not available.

a. From the NOAA Spend Plan after rescissions and sequestration were applied.

b. All OMAO R&D funding is for equipment.

---

[88] Stacy Dennery, NOAA Budget Office, e-mail, August 7, 2013.

Department of Agriculture[89]

U.S. Department of Agriculture (USDA) research and education activities are administered in four of its agencies: Agricultural Research Service (ARS), National Institute of Food and Agriculture (NIFA),[90] Economic Research Service (ERS), and National Agricultural Statistics Service (NASS). The Administration's FY2014 budget request for activities under USDA's Research, Education, and Economics (REE) mission area is $2.81 billion, an increase of 11% from the FY2012 enacted level of $2.54 billion. (See **Table 14**.) The House and Senate committees recommended $2.53 billion and $2.66 billion, respectively. When referring to the Administration's request, Secretary of Agriculture Tom Vilsack stated that

> [A]gricultural research is a proven investment. It is important to increase our investment in research and education, which has proven to be a powerful strategy to boost farm productivity, and has contributed to creation of jobs and enhancing rural economies. As farmers and ranchers face challenges from more frequent and more intense extreme weather conditions, we are focused on providing best practices and workable strategies to adapt to the changes and mitigate the impact.[91]

The Agricultural Research Service is USDA's in-house basic and applied research agency, and operates approximately 90 laboratories nationwide. ARS also includes the National Agricultural Library, a primary information resource on food, agriculture, and natural resource sciences. ARS laboratories focus on efficient food and fiber production, development of new products and uses for agricultural commodities, development of effective controls for pest management, and support of USDA regulatory and technical assistance programs.

The President requested $1.28 billion for ARS in FY2014, $184 million above the FY2012 enacted level. The House and Senate committees recommended $1.07 billion and $1.12 billion, respectively. The FY2014 request proposes $155 million to replace the agency's Southeast Poultry Disease Research Laboratory in Athens, GA. The request fully funds only this single facility rather than making smaller upgrades across multiple facilities. The President also requested funding for additional research to increase the economic value of biorefinery co-products, for example, while proposing to eliminate lower priority extramural projects (particularly for research carried out by other institutions) and to close six selected laboratories. Funding from proposed discontinued ARS projects would be redirected to agency research priorities such as enhanced floral and nursery research, improved feed efficiency and reduced antimicrobial resistance in livestock, and food safety.

The National Institute of Food and Agriculture was established in Title VII, Section 7511 of the Food, Conservation, and Energy Act of 2008 (P.L. 110-246, also known as the 2008 farm bill). NIFA is responsible for developing partnerships between the federal and state components of agricultural research, extension, and institutions of higher education. NIFA distributes funds to

---

[89] This section was written by Dennis A. Shields, Specialist in Agricultural Policy, CRS Resources, Science, and Industry Division.

[90] NIFA was formerly the Cooperative State Research, Education, and Extension Service (CSREES).

[91] U.S. Department of Agriculture, "Statement by Thomas J. Vilsack, Secretary of Agriculture, Before the Subcommittee on Agriculture, Rural Development, Food and Drug Administration, and Related Agencies, Committee on Appropriations, U.S. House of Representatives," April 16, 2013, http://appropriations.house.gov/uploadedfiles/hhrg-113-ap01-wstate-vilsackt-20130416.pdf.

State Agricultural Experiment Stations, State Cooperative Extension Systems, land-grant universities, and other institutions and organizations that conduct agricultural research, education, and outreach. Included in these partnerships is funding for research at 1862 land-grant institutions, 1890 historically black colleges and universities, 1994 tribal land-grant colleges, and Hispanic-serving institutions.[92] Funding is distributed to the states through competitive awards, statutory formula funding, and special grants. The FY2014 request would provide $1.29 billion for NIFA, $86 million above the FY2012 enacted level. The House and Senate committees recommended $1.22 billion and $1.30 billion, respectively.

The Administration's FY2014 request for NIFA emphasizes competitive, peer-reviewed allocation of research funding for what USDA perceives are the most critical needs of agriculture. For FY2014, the President requested $383 million for NIFA's flagship competitive grant program, the Agriculture and Food Research Initiative (AFRI), 45% higher than FY2012 enacted funding of $264 million. AFRI's programs focus on plant and animal health and production, agricultural systems and technologies, bioenergy and natural resources, food safety, human nutrition, and health. Proposed major initiatives in FY2014 include (1) support of schools and colleges in the development of food and agriculture-related workforce; (2) water research to develop solutions for resource management; (3) REE efforts for food security; (4) nutrition and obesity prevention research; (5) food safety research with a focus on minimizing antibiotic resistance transmission through the food chain; (6) biomass research; and (7) strategies for farm production and climate change. To improve transparency and accountability, the President requested $8 million to consolidate and modernize NIFA's grant management systems, which is also expected to help the agency better track research accomplishments.

The President's budget seeks to reorganize several science, technology, engineering, and mathematics (STEM) programs across the executive branch. Under the reorganization, the National Science Foundation would play a leadership role in federal undergraduate and graduate STEM education efforts, the Department of Education would focus on K-12 STEM education, and the Smithsonian Institution would focus on informal STEM education. Under the President's plan, NIFA's STEM education programs would be transferred to these agencies. (For additional information, see "Reorganization of STEM Education Programs.")

The FY2014 budget request proposes $78.5 million for ERS, nearly the same as the FY2012 enacted level. The House and Senate committees recommended $75.5 million and $78.5 million, respectively. ERS supports economic and social science information analysis on agriculture, rural development, food, commodity markets, and the environment. It collects and disseminates data concerning USDA programs and policies to various stakeholders.

Funding for the National Agricultural Statistics Service is proposed at $159 million in the FY2014 request, the same as the FY2012 enacted level. The House and Senate committees recommended $154.8 million and $162.1 million, respectively. The FY2014 request includes new funding to maintain production of four high-priority Current Industry Reports (CIR) that were formerly produced by the U.S. Census Bureau.

---

[92] The numbers 1862, 1890, and 1994 in this context refer to the years laws were enacted creating these classifications of colleges and universities.

Table 14. U.S. Department of Agriculture R&D

(in millions of dollars)

	FY2012 Actual	FY2013 Estimate	FY2014 Request	FY2014 House Committee	FY2014 Senate Committee
Agricultural Research Service					
Product Quality/Value Added	101	n/a	85	n/a	n/a
Livestock Production	76	n/a	73	n/a	n/a
Crop Production	229	n/a	229	n/a	n/a
Food Safety	106	n/a	119	n/a	n/a
Livestock Protection	76	n/a	80	n/a	n/a
Crop Protection	194	n/a	180	n/a	n/a
Human Nutrition	85	n/a	96	n/a	n/a
Environmental Stewardship	189	n/a	220	n/a	n/a
National Agricultural Library	21	n/a	26	n/a	n/a
Repair and Maintenance of Facilities	18	n/a	18	n/a	n/a
Buildings and Facilities	0		155	n/a	n/a
Total, ARS	**1,095**	**1,072**	**1,279**	**1,074**	**1,123**
National Institute of Food and Agriculture					
Smith-Lever Sections 3b&c	294	286	294	294	300
Hatch Act Formula	236	230	236	236	244
1890 Research and Extension	93	n/a	93	93	96
McIntire-Stennis Cooperative Forestry Res.	33	32	33	33	34
Animal Health and Disease Research	4	4	0	4	4
Agriculture and Food Research Initiative	264	290	383	291	316
Pest Management/Crop Protection Act.	32	n/a	29	17	18
Sustainable Agriculture Research and Ext.	19	14	23	19	23
Higher Education Programs	46	n/a	37	n/a	n/a
1890 Facilities	20	n/a	20	20	20
Expanded Food and Nutrition Educ. Prog.	68	n/a	68	68	68
Federal Administration	14	n/a	14	14	n/a
Other	84	n/a	63	n/a	n/a
Total, NIFA	**1,207**	**1,202**	**1,293**	**1,221**	**1,299**
Economic Research Service	**78**	**75**	**79**	**75**	**79**
National Agricultural Statistics Service	**159**	**175**	**159**	**155**	**162**
Total, Research, Education, and Econ.	**2,539**	**2,524**	**2,810**	**2,525**	**2,663**

Sources: For FY2012 data and FY2014 Request, USDA *FY2014 Budget Summary and Annual Performance Plan*, April 2013; for FY2013 Estimate, a rescission of 2.713% is subtracted from amounts in *Explanatory Statement for the Senate Substitute Continuing Resolution* for P.L. 113-6. For FY2014 House Committee data, H.Rept. 113-116, to accompany H.R. 2410. For FY2014 Senate Committee data, S.Rept. 113-46 to accompany S. 1244.

Note: FY2013 estimates exclude deduction for sequestration. n/a = not available. Totals may differ from the sum of the components due to rounding.

Department of the Interior[93]

The Administration has requested $963.1 million in R&D funding for the Department of the Interior (DOI) for FY2014, $143.6 million above its FY2012 funding level of $819.5 million. (See **Table 15**.) According to DOI,

> This funding supports scientific monitoring, research, and analysis to assist decisionmaking in resource management and the special trust responsibilities of Interior and other federally-mandated and nationally-significant programs. Specific activities supported include energy permitting, ecosystem management, oil spill restoration, Earth observations, such as water and wildlife monitoring, invasive species control, and tribal natural resource management.[94]

The U.S. Geological Survey (USGS) accounts for most of DOI's R&D ($760.5 million, 79% of total DOI R&D). USGS is also the most R&D-intensive agency in DOI, with approximately two-thirds of its FY2014 request devoted to R&D activities.

Funding for DOI R&D is generally included in line items that also include non-R&D funding. Therefore it is not possible to know precisely how much of the funding provided for in appropriations bills will be allocated to R&D unless funding is provided for at the precise level of the request. In general, R&D funding levels are known only after DOI agencies determine their allocation of appropriations. In May 2013, DOI provided detailed information to CRS on R&D funding levels proposed by the President for each of its agencies and for broad program areas; these data were used for much of the analysis in this section.[95]

U.S. Geological Survey

All USGS funding is provided through a single account, Surveys, Investigations, and Research (SIR). USGS R&D is conducted under seven SIR activity/program areas: Ecosystems; Climate and Land Use Change; Energy, Minerals, and Environmental Health; Natural Hazards; Water Resources; Core Science Systems; and Administration and Enterprise Information.

The President's FY2014 budget request for USGS is $1.167 billion, and includes $760.5 million for R&D, an increase of $87.7 million (13.0%) over the FY2012 R&D funding level of $672.8 million. The largest R&D increases over FY2012 are for Ecosystems, up $22.5 million (14.2%); Climate and Land Use Change, up $15.3 million (14.9%); and Core Science Systems, up $18.9 million (21.4%).

Other DOI Agencies

Under the President's FY2014 budget request:

---

[93] This section was written by John F. Sargent, Specialist in Science and Technology Policy, CRS Resources, Science, and Industry Division.

[94] Unpublished document, ⬚⬚⬚⬚⬚⬚ ⬚⬚⬚ ⬚ ⬚⬚⬚⬚⬚⬚ ⬚⬚⬚⬚⬚⬚ ⬚⬚⬚⬚⬚⬚⬚⬚⬚ ⬚⬚⬚provided via private email correspondence between the DOI budget office and CRS, May 2, 2013

[95] Private email correspondence between the DOI budget office and CRS, May 2, 2013.

- The U.S. Fish and Wildlife Service would receive $50.1 million in FY2014 for applied research, an increase of $21.6 million (75.6%) over its FY2012 level.

- The Bureau of Ocean Energy Management would receive $39.6 million in FY2014 for applied research, an increase of $1.0 million (2.6%) over FY2012.

- The National Park Service would receive $34.1 million in FY2014 for applied research and development, an increase of $7.8 million (29.7%) over FY2012.

- The Bureau of Safety and Environmental Enforcement would receive $28.0 million in FY2014 for applied research, up $3.3 million (13.2%) over FY2012.

- The Bureau of Land Management would receive $27.1 million in FY2014 for applied research and development, up $10.5 million (63.3%) over FY2012.

- The Bureau of Reclamation would receive $17.6 million in FY2014 for applied research and development, up $5.5 million (45.8%) over FY2012.

- The Bureau of Indian Affairs and the Office of Surface Mining would receive $5.0 million and $1.2 million, respectively, in FY2014 for applied research. Neither agency received R&D funding in FY2012.[96]

Table 15. Department of the Interior R&D

(budget authority, in millions of dollars)

	FY2012 Actual	FY2013 Enacted P.L. 113-6	FY2014 Request
U.S. Geological Survey	672.8	n/a	760.5
Bureau of Land Management	16.6	n/a	27.1
Bureau of Reclamation	12.0	n/a	17.6
National Park Service	26.3	n/a	34.1
Fish and Wildlife Service	28.5	n/a	50.1
Bureau of Ocean Energy Management	38.6	n/a	39.6
Bureau of Safety and Environmental Enforcement	24.7	n/a	28.0
Bureau of Indian Affairs	0	n/a	5.0
Office of Surface Mining	0	n/a	1.2
Total, DOI R&D	**819.5**	n/a	**963.1**

Source: Unpublished data provided to CRS by the DOI Budget Office.

Note: Totals may differ from the sum of the components due to rounding. n/a = not available.

---

[96] Ibid.

Environmental Protection Agency[97]

The U.S. Environmental Protection Agency (EPA), the regulatory agency responsible for carrying out a number of environmental pollution control laws, funds a broad portfolio of research and development activities to provide scientific tools and knowledge to support decisions relating to preventing, regulating, and abating environmental pollution. Beginning in FY2006, EPA has been funded through the Interior, Environment, and Related Agencies appropriations bill. Funding for EPA R&D is generally included in line-items that also include non-R&D funding, therefore it is not possible to identify precisely how much of the funding provided for in appropriations bills will be allocated to R&D (see discussion later in this section). Most of EPA's scientific research activities are funded within the agency's Science and Technology (S&T) appropriations account. This account is funded by a "base" appropriation and a transfer from the Hazardous Substance Superfund (Superfund) account. These transferred funds are dedicated to research on more effective methods to clean up contaminated sites.

The President's FY2014 budget request of $807.5 million for the EPA S&T account, including transfers from the Superfund account, is $9.2 million (1.1%) less than the $816.7 million provided for FY2012 in the Consolidated Appropriations Act, 2012 (P.L. 112-74 Title II of Division E, H.R. 2055) enacted December 23, 2011. The amount included in the FY2014 budget request for the EPA's S&T account (including transfers) represents roughly 10% of the agency's total $8.15 billion request for FY2014. (Note: FY2012 enacted amounts presented in this section of the report reflect the application of a 0.16% rescission.)[98]

The FY2014 request reflects the reorganization of the EPA S&T budget presentation of certain program activities below the appropriations account level as proposed by the Administration and accepted by the Conferees for FY2012.[99] The reorganization included consolidation and modifications of specific line-items, making it difficult to make direct comparisons with the prior fiscal years' enacted levels for sub-account level line-items. Program areas revised as part of the modifications within the S&T account include Clean Air and Climate; Research: Air, Climate and Energy; Research: Chemical Safety and Sustainability; and Research: Sustainability and Healthy Communities.

As indicated in **Table 16**, the total base (prior to transfers) requested funding of $783.9 million for FY2014 for the S&T account is a decrease compared to the FY2012 enacted level. The $23.5 million proposed transfer from the Superfund account for FY2014 is a slight increase above the $23.0 million transferred in FY2012. As indicated in EPA's FY2014 congressional budget

---

[97] This section was written by Robert Esworthy, Specialist in Environmental Policy, CRS Resources, Science, and Industry Division. For a broader overview of EPA's FY2013 appropriations, see CRS Report R42520, ⬜⬜⬜⬜⬜ ⬜⬜⬜⬜ ⬜⬜⬜⬜⬜⬜⬜ ⬜⬜⬜⬜⬜⬜⬜⬜⬜⬜⬜⬜⬜⬜⬜⬜⬜⬜⬜⬜⬜⬜ ⬜⬜⬜⬜⬜ ⬜⬜ ⬜⬜⬜ᵗʰ ⬜⬜⬜⬜⬜⬜, coordinated by Robert Esworthy; for FY2012 see CRS Report R42332, ⬜⬜⬜⬜⬜ ⬜ ⬜⬜⬜⬜⬜⬜⬜⬜⬜⬜⬜ ⬜⬜⬜⬜ ⬜⬜⬜⬜⬜⬜⬜⬜⬜⬜⬜⬜⬜⬜⬜⬜⬜, by Robert Esworthy.

[98] Title IV, Division E of P.L. 112-74, Section 436(a): "Across-the-board Rescissions—There is hereby rescinded an amount equal to 0.16 percent of the budget authority provided for fiscal year 2012 for any discretionary appropriation in titles I through IV of this Act." FY2012 enacted amounts presented in EPA's FY2013 Congressional Budget Justification include the subsequent application of the rescission. The total FY2012 enacted appropriations for the EPA S&T account, including transfers, in P.L. 112-74 was $818.0 million prior to the rescission.

[99] Reorganized as proposed by the President for FY2012, U.S. EPA ⬜⬜⬜⬜⬜⬜⬜⬜⬜⬜⬜⬜⬜⬜ ⬜⬜⬜⬜⬜⬜⬜⬜⬜ ⬜⬜⬜⬜⬜⬜⬜⬜⬜⬜⬜ ⬜⬜⬜⬜ ⬜⬜⬜ ⬜⬜⬜⬜⬜ ⬜⬜⬜ ⬜ ⬜⬜⬜⬜ ⬜⬜ ⬜⬜⬜⬜⬜⬜⬜⬜⬜⬜⬜⬜⬜⬜⬜⬜⬜ ⬜⬜⬜ ⬜⬜⬜⬜⬜⬜⬜⬜⬜⬜⬜⬜, available on EPA's Historical Planning, Budget, and Results Reports website at http://www2.epa.gov/planandbudget/archive.

justification[100] and reflected in **Table 16**, the requested base amount for the S&T account includes both increases and decreases of varying levels for the individual EPA research program and activity line-items identified within the account when compared with the enacted FY2012 appropriations. For some activities, the amount of the request for FY2014 remained relatively flat compared to the FY2012 appropriation.

Examples of FY2014 requested reductions below the FY2012 levels, as reflected in **Table 16** for programmatic areas within EPA's S&T appropriations account, include $147.4 million for Sustainable and Healthy Communities (human health and ecosystem) Research, $26.2 million (roughly 15%) less than FY2012 enacted; and $40.0 million for FY2014 for EPA's Homeland Security research activities,[101] $1.8 million (4.2%) less than FY2012.

The largest requested percentage decrease for FY2014 below FY2012 enacted levels within the S&T account is for the Climate Protection Program activity within the Clean Air and Climate program area. The $8.3 million requested for the Climate Protection Program for FY2014 is $8.0 million (nearly 50%) less than the FY2012 appropriation of $16.3 million.[102] The requested decrease reflects the Administration's proposal to eliminate the vehicle engine development under the Clean Automotive Technology (CAT) program, and reallocate funds that previously supported the CAT to support implementation and compliance activities associated with EPA's new greenhouse gas (GHG) emission standards and National Highway Traffic Safety Administration (NHTSA) Corporate Average Fuel Economy (CAFE) fuel economy standards and EPA emission standards for light-duty and heavy-duty vehicles and engines. The funding for this activity— Federal Vehicle and Fuel Standards and Certification—is also within the Clean Air and Climate program area: $100.4 million for FY2014, an $8.5 million (9.2%) increase above the FY2012 enacted amount.

Additionally within the S&T account, the FY2014 request includes $105.7 million for Air, Climate, and Energy (ACE) Research, a $7.8 million (7.8%) increase above FY2012, and $117.9 million for Safe and Sustainable Water (SSW) Research, a $5.1 million (4.4%) increase. Primarily contributing to these two requested increases are $3.8 million and $4.3 million increases requested above FY2012 under ACE and SWW research program activities respectively, as part of EPA's overall research efforts to address questions regarding the safety of hydraulic fracturing.[103] Concerns regarding potential drinking water impacts associated with hydraulic fracturing continue to be an area of considerable interest during the 113th Congress.[104]

Additional examples of increases and reductions within the S&T account activities highlighted in the EPA FY2014 Congressional Budget Justification and supporting documents[105] include the following:

---

[100] U.S. EPA ▢▢▢▢▢▢▢▢▢▢▢▢ ▢▢▢▢▢▢▢▢▢ ▢▢▢▢▢▢▢▢▢▢▢ ▢▢▢▢ ▢▢▢▢▢▢▢ ▢▢▢ ▢ ▢▢▢▢ ▢▢ ▢▢▢▢▢▢▢▢▢▢▢
▢▢▢▢▢▢ ▢▢▢ ▢▢▢▢▢▢▢pp. 72-199, http://www2.epa.gov/sites/production/files/documents/cjfy14.pdf.

[101] Under the Bioterrorism Act of 2002, and Homeland Security Presidential Directives 7, 9, and 10, EPA is the lead federal agency for coordinating security of the nation's water systems, and plays a role in developing early warning monitoring and decontamination capabilities associated with potential attacks using biological contaminants.

[102] See footnote 100, EPA's FY2014 Congressional Justification, pdf, pp. 84-85.

[103] See footnote 100, EPA's FY2014 Congressional Justification, pdf, pp. 36, 151-154, and 160-165.

[104] CRS Report R41760, ▢▢▢▢▢▢▢▢▢▢▢▢▢ ▢▢▢ ▢▢▢▢ ▢▢▢▢▢ ▢ ▢▢▢▢▢▢▢▢▢▢▢▢ ▢▢▢▢, by Mary Tiemann and Adam Vann.

[105] See FY2014 Congressional Justification, and "FY2014 EPA Budget in Brief," http://www2.epa.gov/planandbudget/
(continued...)

- $4.1 million increase for research to develop processes and products that minimize the hazardous impacts of the manufacture, use, and disposal of chemicals, including nanomaterials;

- $3.2 million increase for climate change research to understand the impacts of climate change on human health and vulnerable ecosystems;

- $1.8 million increase to support development of regional projects that integrate natural and engineered water infrastructure as well as research to monitor effects of existing integrated natural, engineered, and green infrastructure;

- $1.3 million increase to expand understanding of the potential impacts of biofuel production on human health and ecosystems;

- $16.4 million decrease from Science to Achieve Results (STAR)/Greater Research Opportunities (GRO) fellowships, as part of the Administration's proposal for reorganization and consolidation of science, technology, engineering, and mathematics (STEM) education programs[106] to facilitate a national unified strategy for federal education fellowships and scholarships;[107]

- $2.3 million decrease from drinking water research including center for research on small drinking water systems competitive grants and drinking water and water quality research for technical support activities; and

- $1.2 million decrease for endocrine disruptors research.

The activities funded within the S&T account include research conducted by universities, foundations, and other non-federal entities that receive EPA grants, and research conducted by the agency at its own laboratories and facilities. R&D at EPA headquarters and laboratories around the country, as well as external R&D, is managed primarily by EPA's Office of Research and Development (ORD). A large portion of the S&T account funds EPA's R&D activities managed by ORD, including the agency's research laboratories and research grants. The account also provides funding for the agency's applied science and technology activities conducted through its program offices (e.g., the Office of Water). Many of the programs implemented by other offices within EPA have a research component, but the research is not necessarily the primary focus of the program.

The EPA S&T account incorporates elements of the former EPA Research and Development account, as well as a portion of the former Salaries and Expenses, and Program Operations accounts, which had been in place until FY1996.[108] Although the Office of Management and

---

(...continued)

fy2014.

[106] See White House Office of Science and Technology, April 10, 2013, Press Release: the FY2014 Federal R&D Budget, http://www.whitehouse.gov/sites/default/files/microsites/ostp/2014_R&Dbudget_STEM.pdf. See also http://www.whitehouse.gov/administration/eop/ostp/rdbudgets.

[107] See footnote 100 EPA's FY2014 Congressional Justification, pp. 172 and 176, http://www2.epa.gov/sites/production/files/documents/cjfy14.pdf.

[108] In recent years, EPA's annual appropriations have been requested, considered, and enacted according to eight statutory appropriations accounts established by Congress during the FY1996 appropriations process. Because of the differences in the scope of the activities included in these accounts, apt comparisons before and after FY1996 are difficult.

Budget (OMB) reports[109] historical and projected budget authority (BA) amounts for R&D at EPA (and other federal agencies), OMB documents do not describe how these amounts explicitly relate to the requested and appropriated funding amounts for the many specific EPA program activities. The R&D BA amounts reported by OMB are typically significantly less than amounts appropriated/requested for the S&T account as a whole. (BA as reported by OMB is included in **Table 16** for purposes of comparison to fiscal year appropriations.) This is an indication that not all of the EPA S&T account funding is allocated to R&D.

No bill providing regular appropriations for FY2014 for Interior, Environment, and Related Agencies has been introduced in the House or Senate (as of August 22, 2013). On July 31, 2013, the House Appropriations Committee began, but did not conclude, a markup of a draft FY2014 appropriations bill. The markup focused on the draft bill text and accompanying draft committee report language approved on July 23, 2013, by the House Appropriations Subcommittee on Interior, Environment, and Related Agencies.[110] In addition, on August 1, 2013, the leaders of the Senate Appropriations Subcommittee on Interior, Environment, and Related Agencies released a draft bill for FY2014 with an accompanying explanatory statement.[111] According to a joint statement released by the Chairman and Ranking Member of the Senate Subcommittee, the draft document is intended to "serve as a meaningful start as discussions continue to finalize a fiscally responsible, balanced FY 2014 Interior bill."[112] The House Subcommittee draft would provide $636.1 million for EPA's S&T account, and the Senate Subcommittee leadership draft recommended $791.0 million.

---

[109] The Office of Management and Budget (OMB) reports R&D budget authority (BA) amounts in its Analytical Perspectives accompanying the annual President's budget request. See OMB, □□□□□□□□□□□ □□□□□□□□□□ □□□□ □□□□□□□□□□□□□□□□□□□□□ □□□□□□□□□□□□□□□□ □□ □ □□□□□□ □□pp. 369-375, http://www.whitehouse.gov/sites/default/files/omb/budget/fy2014/assets/topics.pdf.

[110] The draft bill text is posted on the House Committee on Appropriations website at http://appropriations.house.gov/uploadedfiles/bills-113hr-fc-ap-fy2014-ap00-interior.pdf. The draft committee report is posted on the House Committee on Appropriations website at http://appropriations.house.gov/uploadedfiles/hrpt-113-hr-fy2014-interior.pdf.

[111] The draft bill text is posted on the Senate Committee on Appropriations website at http://www.appropriations.senate.gov/news.cfm?method=news.view&id=b3e22f9d-a060-45eb-90ef-1225244125a7. The explanatory statement is posted on the Senate Committee on Appropriations website at http://www.appropriations.senate.gov/news.cfm?method=news.view&id=d1037190-bf9c-420c-a8a5-79c0ef9c495c.

[112] Committee on Appropriations, U.S. Senate, "Reed and Murkowski Release Draft of FY2014 Interior, Environment, and Related Agencies Appropriation Bill," press release, August 1, 2013, http://www.appropriations.senate.gov/customcf/uploads/2a912190-bbd9-4a71-806e-380da102c96e/080113%20Interior%20Press%20Release%20-%20FINAL.pdf.

Table 16. Environmental Protection Agency S&T Account

(in millions of dollars)

Environmental Protection Agency	FY2012 Enacted (P.L. 112-74)	FY2013 Enacted (P.L. 113-6)a	FY2014 Request
Science and Technology Approps. Account			
Clean Air and Climate	124.4	n/a	126.0
- *Climate Protection Program*	*16.3*	*n/a*	*8.3*
- *Federal Vehicle & Fuel Standards & Certification*	*91.9*	*n/a*	*100.4*
Enforcement	15.3	n/a	15.9
Homeland Security	41.8	n/a	40.0
Indoor Air and Radiation	6.8	n/a	6.7
IT/Data Management/Security	3.7	n/a	4.0
Operations & Administration	72.0	n/a	75.7
Pesticide Licensing	6.6	n/a	6.2
Research: Air, Climate, and Energy	98.0	n/a	105.7
Research: Safe and Sustainable Water	112.8	n/a	117.9
Research: Chemical Safety and Sustainability	130.2	n/a	134.8
- *Research: Computational toxicology*	*20.8*	*n/a*	*21.4*
- *Research: Endocrine disruptor*	*16.9*	*n/a*	*15.9*
- *Research: Fellowships*	*16.4*	*n/a*	*0.0*
Research: Sustainable and Healthy Communities	173.5	n/a	147.4
Water: Human Health Protection	3.8	n/a	3.6
Research: National Priorities (Water Quality and Availability)	5.0	n/a	0.0
—Subtotal S&T Account Base Appropriations	**$793.7**	**n/a**	**$783.9**
—Transfer in from Hazardous Substance Superfund Account	**$23.0**	**n/a**	**$23.5**
Total Science and Technology	**$816.7**	**n/a**	**$807.5**
R&D Budget Authority Reported by OMB	*$568.0*	*n/a*	*$560.0 est.*

Source: Prepared by CRS. FY2012 enacted amounts are as presented by the House Appropriations Committee in its report accompanying the Interior, Environment, and Related Agencies Appropriations Bill, 2013 (H.R. 6091, H.Rept. 112-589, pp. 170-177), as reported July 10, 2012, and reflect the subsequent application of the 0.16% across-the-board rescission required by Section 436 of P.L. 112-74. FY2014 requested amounts are based on the *Fiscal year FY2014 Justification of Appropriation Estimates for the Committee on Appropriations: Science and Technology,* http://www2.epa.gov/sites/production/files/documents/cjfy14.pdf. OMB amounts of R&D budget authority are as reported in OMB, *Fiscal Year 2014 Budget of the United States: Analytical Perspectives—Special Topics/Research and Development,* pp. 369-375, http://www.whitehouse.gov/sites/default/files/omb/budget/fy2014/assets/topics.pdf.

Notes: Totals may differ from the sum of the components due to rounding; n/a=not available.

a.   FY2013 enacted amounts will be added to the table following agencies and departments' submissions to the House and Senate Appropriations Committees pursuant to Section 113 Title I Div. F of P.L. 113-6, reporting allocations at the program, project or activity level within each statutory account and reflecting the effects of sequestration and rescissions.

Department of Transportation[113]

President Obama has requested $940.6 million for Department of Transportation R&D in FY2014, an increase of $20.3 million (2.2%) from the FY2012 enacted level. (See **Table 17**.) Two DOT agencies—the Federal Highway Administration (FHWA) and the Federal Aviation Administration (FAA)—account for more than three-fourths of the department's R&D funding (76.6% in the FY2014 request).

The FHWA would receive $379.8 million in R&D funding in FY2014 under the President's request, a decrease of $26.1 million (6.4%) from the FY2012 enacted level.[114] The FHWA budget proposes to restructure its existing research, development, and technology activities into three programs, as authorized by the Moving Ahead for Progress in the 21st Century Act (MAP-21, P.L. 112-141): Highway Research and Development (HRD), Technology and Innovation Deployment, and Training and Education. The President's FY2014 request includes $115 million for HRD. The House Committee on Appropriations recommended the requested amount for FHWA. The Senate Committee on Appropriations also recommended the requested amount for FHWA, plus an additional $500 million for bridges in critical condition.[115]

As in the President's FY2013 budget request for the FHWA, the FY2014 request would transfer the functions of the Research and Innovative Technology Administration (RITA) to a new office, the Office of the Assistant Secretary for Research and Technology. Funding for RITA in the FY2014 budget request appears in the account for the Office of the Secretary. The department asserts that the establishment of the new office would "improve coordination and collaboration among operating administrations, resulting in higher quality research outcomes." Activities to be administered by this office include Intelligent Transportation Systems ($100 million in the FY2014 request), University Transportation Centers ($72.5 million), and the Bureau of Transportation Statistics ($26 million).[116] The House committee endorsed the President's proposal to move RITA to the Office of the Secretary under the direction of an Assistant Secretary for Research and Technology, instead of a separate administrator. The House committee recommended $14.2 million for the new office, $545,000 below the President's request. The new office would be responsible for

> coordinating, facilitating, and reviewing the Department's research and development programs and activities; coordinating and developing positioning, navigation and timing (PNT) technology; maintaining PNT policy, coordination and spectrum management; managing the Nationwide Differential Global Positioning System; and overseeing and providing direction to the Bureau of Transportation Statistics, the Intelligent Transportation Systems Joint Program Office, the University Transportation Centers program, the Volpe National Transportation Systems Center and the Transportation Safety Institute.[117]

---

[113] This section was written by John F. Sargent, Specialist in Science and Technology Policy, CRS Resources, Science, and Industry Division.

[114] FHWA, ░░░░░░░░░░░ ░░░░░░░░░░░░░░░░░░░░░░░░ ░░░░░░░ ░░░░░░░░░░, http://www.dot.gov/sites/dot.dev/files/docs/FHWA_FY2014_Budget_Estimates_0.pdf.

[115] S.Rept. 113-45, p. 42.

[116] U.S. Department of Transportation, ░░░░░░ ░░░░░░░░░░░░░░░░░░░░, http://www.dot.gov/sites/dot.dev/files/docs/OST_FY2014_Budget_EstimatesV2_0.pdf, p. 1.

[117] H.Rept. 113-136, p. 8.

The Senate committee also endorsed the President's proposal to move RITA to the Office of the Secretary under the direction of an Assistant Secretary for Research and Technology, recommending funding of $14.8 million, the same as the President's request.[118]

The FAA budget justification reflects a request for $340.7 million for R&D and R&D facilities in FY2014, a decrease of $26.0 million (7.1%) from the FY2012 enacted level.[119] The request includes $166.0 million for Research, Engineering, and Development (RE&D), a decrease of $1.5 million (0.9%) from the FY2012 level. The RE&D budget is focused on improving aviation safety, economic competitiveness, and environmental sustainability. The request includes $90.9 million for safety, up 1.8% over FY2012; $35.8 million for economic competitiveness, up 4.8% over FY2012; and $33.5 million for environmental sustainability, down 13.1%. The FAA request includes $61.4 million in funding for NextGen in the RE&D account, an increase of 2%. The RE&D NextGen-specific funding supports research in wake turbulence, human factors, and clean aircraft technologies.[120] The House committee recommended $145.0 million for RE&D, $21.0 million below the President's request; the Senate committee recommended $160.0 million for RE&D, $6 million below the request. The House recommended no funding for the Joint Planning and Development Office (JPDO) stating that the "FAA has failed to establish a clearly defined role for the JPDO."[121] The Senate recommended $9.0 million for JPDO, $3.1 million below the request. The House committee also recommended less than the President's request for NextGen activities in wake turbulence (down $4.3 million, 46%), air ground integration human factors (down $5.8 million, 56%), and weather technology in the cockpit (down $1.2 million, 28%), and more for NextGen environmental research in aircraft technologies, fuels, and metrics (up $3.0 million, 16%).[122] The Senate recommended some reductions in the NextGen activities cut by the House, and recommended $2.4 million more than the request for NextGen environmental research.[123]

Funding for Federal Railroad Administration R&D would more than double under the President's FY2014 proposal to $90.8 million, an increase of $51.1 million (128.7%) above the FY2012 level. This increase is due primarily to the proposed establishment of a new account (the Research, Development, and Technology account) which would support high-performance rail R&D ($24.5 million), a National Cooperative Research Program ($5.0 million), and Workforce Development R&D-related activities ($24.8 million).[124] The House committee recommended the requested amount ($35.3 million) for the Railroad Research and Development account, but recommended no funding for the Administration's proposed Railroad Research, Development, and Technology account noting that "it has not received formal legislative proposal for such program."[125] The Senate committee also recommended the requested amount for the Railroad

---

[118] S.Rept. 113-45, p. 21.

[119] FAA, ▯▯▯▯▯▯▯▯▯▯▯ ▯▯▯▯▯▯▯▯▯▯▯▯▯▯▯▯▯▯▯▯▯▯▯▯▯▯▯▯▯ ▯▯▯ ▯▯▯▯▯▯▯▯▯, http://www.dot.gov/sites/dot.dev/files/docs/FAA_FY2014_Budget_Estimates.pdf.

[120] Ibid.

[121] H.Rept. 113-136, p. 28.

[122] Ibid, p. 28.

[123] S.Rept. 113-45, p. 37.

[124] FRA, ▯▯▯▯▯▯▯▯▯▯▯ ▯▯▯▯▯▯▯▯▯▯▯▯▯▯▯▯▯▯▯▯▯▯▯▯▯▯▯▯▯ ▯▯▯ ▯▯▯▯▯▯▯▯▯, http://www.dot.gov/sites/dot.dev/files/docs/FRA_FY2014_Budget_Estimates.pdf,

[125] H.Rept. 113-136, p. 44.

Research and Development account and recommended no funding for the Administration's proposed Railroad Research, Development, and Technology account.[126]

Federal Transit Administration R&D would more than double to $17.2 million, an increase of $10.2 million (152.4%) over FY2012. This is due primarily to congressional redirection of funding for the Research, Development, Demonstration, and Deployment account to support R&D activities in contrast to its FY2012 funding support for technology investments.[127] The House recommended $20.0 million for the Research, Development, Demonstration, and Deployment account, $10.0 million below the President's request. In addition to the authorities given to the FTA under MAP-21, the House committee provides FTA authorization to "award grants to demonstrate and deploy new technologies that promote clean energy and improve air quality with low-emission or no-emission vehicles."[128] The Senate committee recommended $43.3 million for the Research, Development, Demonstration, and Deployment account, $13.3 million above the President's request.[129]

Table 17. Department of Transportation R&D

(budget authority, in millions of dollars)

	FY2012 Actual	FY2013 Enacted (P.L. 113-6)	FY2014 Request	FY2014 House Committee	FY2014 Senate Committee
Federal Highway Administration	405.9	n/a	379.8	n/a	n/a
Federal Aviation Administration	366.7	n/a	340.7	n/a	n/a
Federal Railroad Administration	39.7	n/a	90.8	n/a	n/a
National Highway Traffic Safety Administration	68.7	n/a	73.4	n/a	n/a
Federal Transit Administration	6.8	n/a	17.2	n/a	n/a
Pipeline & Hazardous Materials Safety Administration	9.8	n/a	16.4	n/a	n/a
Office of the Secretary	16.0	n/a	14.8	n/a	n/a
Federal Motor Carrier Safety Administration	6.7	n/a	7.5	n/a	n/a
Total, DOT R&D	**920.4**	n/a	**940.6**	n/a	n/a

Source: DOT FY2014 department and agency budget justifications.

Notes: Figures include R&D and R&D facilities. n/a = not available. Totals may differ from the sum of the components due to rounding. Research and development funds are included in accounts that also have non-R&D activities.

---

[126] S.Rept. 113-45, p. 189.

[127] Congress articulated the new direction in MAP-21, the Moving Ahead for Progress in the 21st Century Act (P.L. 112-141).

[128] H.Rept. 113-136, p. 54.

[129] S.Rept. 113-45, p. 80.

Author Contact Information

John F. Sargent Jr., Coordinator
Specialist in Science and Technology Policy
jsargent@crs.loc.gov, 7-9147

Robert Esworthy
Specialist in Environmental Policy
resworthy@crs.loc.gov, 7-7236

Heather B. Gonzalez
Specialist in Science and Technology Policy
hgonzalez@crs.loc.gov, 7-1895

Daniel Morgan
Specialist in Science and Technology Policy
dmorgan@crs.loc.gov, 7-5849

John D. Moteff
Specialist in Science and Technology Policy
jmoteff@crs.loc.gov, 7-1435

Wendy H. Schacht
Specialist in Science and Technology Policy
wschacht@crs.loc.gov, 7-7066

Pamela W. Smith
Analyst in Biomedical Policy
psmith@crs.loc.gov, 7-7048

Harold F. Upton
Analyst in Natural Resources Policy
hupton@crs.loc.gov, 7-2264

Dennis A. Shields
Specialist in Agricultural Policy
dshields@crs.loc.gov, 7-9051